The National
Literacy Strategy

Spelling bank
Lists of words and activities
for the KS2 spelling objectives

**Department for
Education and Employment**

Contents

Department for Education and Employment
Sanctuary Buildings
Great Smith Street
London SW1P 3BT

© Crown copyright 1999

Extracts from this document may be reproduced for non-commercial
educational or training purposes on condition that the source is acknowledged.

ISBN 0 19 312240 5

Introduction

This booklet contains lists of words and ideas to help in the teaching of the Key Stage 2 spelling objectives set out in the *National Literacy Strategy Framework for Teaching*. They are drawn from the Word Level strand, predominantly from the section entitled 'Spelling Rules and Conventions', but with a few from the 'Vocabulary Extension' objectives.

A page is devoted to each individual objective, although there are obvious links between objectives, particularly those covering prefixes, suffixes, roots and modified endings. To ensure a smooth incline in learning, you will find it useful to look at examples from previous and later year groups to see how these strands develop.

The word lists are not exhaustive; they have been selected as the most common and appropriate words for the age group, and the most useful for teaching. Families of words have been represented by a single word rather than listing every variation.

Some objectives are revisited or, more accurately, approached from different angles. For example, the choices involved in putting **s** onto the end of a word are tackled as part of pluralisation, tense and the use of suffixes. This is a deliberate attempt to anchor key rules securely.

For each objective you will find not only a bank of useful words, but suggestions for teaching the objective in whole-class and group time. At the bottom of each page you will usually find notes which include the rules or conventions themselves.

For more specific ideas and lesson materials, look in the orange National Literacy Strategy booklet for Module 2 'Word Level Work: Activity Resource Sheets'. For information, call 01536 741171 or visit our web site at www.standards.dfee.gov.uk.

This booklet is issued as an extra support to the National Literacy Strategy training materials for 1999–2000, which include a 1.5 hour session on spelling for each year of Key Stage 2. Contact your Local Education Authority's Literacy Consultant/s for further details. Extracts from the training which may prove useful have been provided in the Appendices.

Year 3 objectives

Year 3 Term 1

Objective 8

How the spellings of verbs alter when **ing** is added

Whole-class approaches
◆ Collect up a list of **ing** words and their base words to compare. Investigate the effect of adding **ing** to the words in the 'ending in **e**' and 'short vowels' lists.
◆ Provide some base words and ask children to add **ing** on individual whiteboards to show you.

Group task
◆ Card-sorting activities.

Extension activity (very challenging)
◆ Add **ing** to words ending in
  – **c** (add in a **k**);
  – vowel + **y** (just add);
  – **l** (double the **l**).

Typical words		Words ending in **e**		Words with short vowels	
help	helping	hope	hoping	hop	hopping
ask	asking	take	taking	run	running
see	seeing	write	writing	shut	shutting
do	doing	drive	driving	chat	chatting
spend	spending	decide	deciding	clap	clapping
go	going	make	making	shop	shopping
enjoy	enjoying	care	caring	plan	planning
lead	leading	stare	staring	rub	rubbing
pull	pulling	hate	hating	slip	slipping
look	looking	like	liking	fit	fitting
jump	jumping	smile	smiling	tip	tipping
meet	meeting	come	coming	bet	betting
say	saying	ride	riding	win	winning
try	trying	amaze	amazing	sit	sitting
walk	walking	raise	raising	slim	slimming

Notes
◆ Most words just add **ing**.
◆ Words ending in **e** drop the **e** to add **ing**.
◆ Words with a short vowel before the final letter double the final letter.

Year 3
Term 1

Objective 9

To investigate and learn to use the spelling pattern **le** as in *little, muddle, bottle, scramble, cradle*

Whole-class approaches

◆ Collect a list of **le** words over time, from shared text or by brainstorming. Investigate the list for familiar patterns, particularly for the letters that tend to precede the **le**.
◆ Experiment in adding suffixes such as **ly**, **ing**, and draw attention to the dropping of the **e**.

Group tasks

◆ Sort the list of words into family groups, e.g. those preceded by double letters, those preceded by **ck**, etc.
◆ Word-hunt for more examples.
◆ Word-hunt for **el** and **al** words.

ckle	able	Double letter + **le**		cle	dle
chuckle	able	middle	ripple	uncle	candle
prickle	table	giggle	nettle	article	handle
tickle	vegetable	guzzle	bottle	cycle	needle
cackle	fable	toggle	muddle	icicle	noodle
trickle	cable	kettle	hobble	obstacle	poodle
pickle	reliable	cattle	puddle	miracle	bundle
	probable	stubble	cuddle	circle	
		little	wriggle	particle	
		bubble	rubble	cubicle	
		apple	nozzle	bicycle	
		ripple	sizzle		
		saddle	wobble		
		paddle	fiddle		

ble	ible	ple
double	sensible	example
trouble	responsible	dimple
bible	possible	simple
fable	horrible	crumple
humble	terrible	ample
tumble		sample
grumble		
rumble		

Notes

◆ **le** is much more common than **el** or **al**.
◆ It is easy to distinguish between **cel** and **cle** because the **c** is always soft in the former and hard in the latter. (Compare *parcel* and *particle*).
◆ The vast majority of **le** endings are preceded by letters which feature an ascender or descender.
◆ **al** words include *pedal, metal, cannibal, medal, petal,* and the **al** suffix appears in words like *medical* and *magical*.
◆ **el** was originally a suffix meaning *small*. Examples include *satchel, label, model, angel, parcel, quarrel, cancel, excel, channel, funnel* and *tunnel*.
◆ There are a huge number of other **le** words which are part of a split digraph, e.g. *sale, tale, whole, mile,* etc. These have been excluded from the list. This particular **le** ending does not produce an extra syllable in the way it does in the list above.

Year 3 Term 1

Objective 10

To recognise and spell common prefixes and how these influence word meanings, e.g. **un**, **de**, **dis**, **re**, **pre**

Whole-class approaches

◆ Use magnetic letters to form prefixes for pre-written words on whiteboard; slide them into place and ask how the prefixes have changed the meaning of the words, and what the prefix means.
◆ Make sets of prefixes and words, hand them out and get children to find a 'partner'. Break the pairs and ask them to find new partners. Each child keeps a note of words created until they have done as many as they can. Compare lists.
◆ Generate words using the same prefix.

Group tasks

◆ Play Kim's game – using 30 assorted word cards from the list below, children hunt for pairs in turns and use checklist for answers.
◆ Investigate other prefixes, working out the meaning of the prefix.

Extension activities

◆ Play Definitions game – children provide a definition and challenge the class to find the right word.
◆ Find words using the letter sequence but not as a prefix, e.g. *disturb, devil, read, preach* and *uncle*.

un	de	dis	re	pre
unable	demist	dishearten	rebound	precaution
unwell	deform	dislike	rebuild	predict
unhappy	decamp	dislodge	recycle	previous
untidy	decode	disown	recall	premature
untrained	defuse	displease	refill	preface
unlucky	deflate	disqualify	reform	prefix
unpopular	debug	disappoint	retreat	prepare
unpick	de-ice	disagree	recede	
unseen	decompose	disappear	return	
unusual		disconnect	replace	
undo		dishonest	revisit	
untie		disinfect	replay	
unzip		disembark	rewrite	
unofficial		disobey	repay	

Notes

◆ The word *prefix* has the prefix **pre**, and can help in your definition.
◆ **un** means 'not'; **de** means 'making the opposite of'; **dis** means 'not', 'the opposite of'; **re** means 'again'; **pre** means 'before'.
◆ A hyphen sometimes appears between the prefix and the word, e.g. *de-ice*.

Year 3 Term 1

Objective 11

To use their knowledge of prefixes to generate new words from root words, especially antonyms, *happy/unhappy, appear/disappear*

Whole-class approaches

◆ Write pairs of words (*happy/unhappy*) in random order on the whiteboard – children sort and define how the antonym has been created.
◆ Play Make an Antonym game, using flashcards from the lists of words without prefixes below.
◆ Place Post-It notes over prefixes in antonyms in shared texts – ask children to work out the appropriate choice, or hold up correct prefix from a selection.

Group tasks

◆ Play Kim's game – place cards upside down and hunt out the pairs of words and their opposites.
◆ Using prefixes covered so far, have the children select one and write down an antonym – three pairs of children in a group in a Beat-the-Clock activity.

Extension activities

◆ Children select an antonym, then come up with synonyms – e.g. *unhappy, miserable, depressed; unseen, invisible, camouflaged*.
◆ Children prepare dominoes – antonym one side, synonym on the other – to be used by other groups.

un		dis		others	
well	unwell	appear	disappear	sense	nonsense
tidy	untidy	arm	disarm	stick	non-stick
usual	unusual	agree	disagree	fiction	non-fiction
certain	uncertain	approve	disapprove	clockwise	anti-clockwise
friendly	unfriendly	connect	disconnect	frost	defrost
do	undo	honest	dishonest	compose	decompose
able	unable	like	dislike	place	misplace
selfish	unselfish	please	displease	behave	misbehave
seen	unseen	qualify	disqualify	possible	impossible
kind	unkind	allow	disallow	probable	improbable
pleasant	unpleasant	comfort	discomfort	regular	irregular
popular	unpopular	trust	distrust	legal	illegal
happy	unhappy	order	disorder	sensitive	insensitive
fair	unfair	obey	disobey	visible	invisible
lucky	unlucky	continue	discontinue	convenient	inconvenient

Notes

◆ Just add the prefix – a no-nonsense rule. This accounts for the double **n** in *unnecessary* and the double **s** in *dissatisfied*.
◆ Useful for handwriting practice.
◆ Stressing the meaning of prefixes is a support for spelling and vocabulary.

Year 3
Term 2

Objective 8 (1 of 2)

How words change when **er** and **est** are added

Whole-class approach

1 >
- Identify words ending in **er** and **est** in Shared Reading/Writing – show how changing the suffix changes the meaning.

2) *discuss rules (see below)*

Group tasks

- Play a matching game – base words have to be paired with suffixes. Position additional function cards (e.g. 'Take away the final **e**') between base words and suffixes where appropriate.
3)
- Investigation – find words that end with **er** and **est** and group them according to the spelling rule. *write in books.*

Extension activities

- Find exceptions, e.g. *good, better, best; bad, worse, worst; far, farther, farthest*.
- Investigate the use of *more* and *most*, e.g. *more curious, more intelligent, more sensible*.

Typical words			e words		
quick	quicker	quickest	nice	nicer	nicest
cold	colder	coldest	late	later	latest
long	longer	longest	close	closer	closest
tall	taller	tallest	ripe	riper	ripest
rich	richer	richest	rude	ruder	rudest

Short (rap) vowels			y words		
big	bigger	biggest	happy	happier	happiest
hot	hotter	hottest	chilly	chillier	chilliest
thin	thinner	thinnest	funny	funnier	funniest
fat	fatter	fattest	crazy	crazier	craziest
			lucky	luckier	luckiest

Notes

- Most words just add **er** and **est**.
- Words ending in **e** drop the **e** and take the suffix.
- Words containing a short vowel before the final consonant double the consonant.
- Words ending in **y** change **y** to **i** to add the suffix.

Year 3
Term 2

Objective 8 (2 of 2)

How words change
when **y** is added

Whole-class approaches

◆ Identify words ending in **y** in Shared Reading/Writing – show how
  changing the suffix changes the meaning.
◆ Children attempt words on individual whiteboards and then show them.
◆ Investigate why some base words drop **e** or double their consonants when
  y is added. See below.

Group task

◆ Find further examples.

Typical words		Short word, short (rap) vowel		e words	
crisp	crispy	fun	funny	grease	greasy
smell	smelly	fur	furry	haze	hazy
cheek	cheeky	fat	fatty	laze	lazy
water	watery	run	runny	bone	bony
fuss	fussy	nut	nutty	smoke	smoky
full	fully	sun	sunny	stone	stony

Notes

◆ Most words just add **y**.
◆ Double the final consonant if it is preceded by a short (rap) vowel.
◆ Words ending in digraph **e** drop the **e** to add the **y**.

Year 3 Term 2

Objective 9

To investigate and identify basic rules for changing the spelling of nouns when **s** is added

Whole-class approaches

◆ Investigation – use word lists or card-sorting. Work out the rules.
◆ Clap out syllables for children to work out if they can hear the extra syllable, and thus add **es** (see the second of the *Notes* below).
◆ Use flashcards for **s** and **es** – ask children to hold up the correct ending for words given.

Group task

◆ Play card games like Gin Rummy in which singulars that use the same ending are collected up.

Extension activity

◆ Plural investigations
   – words ending in vowels (**es** unless preceded by another vowel);
   – words ending in **f** (**ff** add **s**; **f** or **fe** use **ves**);
   – plurals that don't use **s** at all, e.g. *children, men, women, teeth, oxen, geese, feet, deer, fish, sheep, mice, dice, lice, larvae, antennae,* etc.

Words as starting points for investigation

ash	ashes	box	boxes	brush	brushes
bush	bushes	church	churches	dish	dishes
glass	glasses	inch	inches	kiss	kisses
inch	inches	sandwich	sandwiches	tax	taxes
watch	watches	fox	foxes	witch	witches
game	games	rope	ropes	shoe	shoes
table	tables	time	times	tune	tunes
pen	pens	bean	beans	tick	ticks
cup	cups	pocket	pockets	school	schools
pond	ponds	window	windows	lip	lips
book	books	desk	desks	clasp	clasps
army	armies	party	parties	baby	babies
berry	berries	city	cities	fly	flies
jelly	jellies	penny	pennies	puppy	puppies
boy	boys	toy	toys	key	keys
ray	rays	display	displays	monkey	monkeys
delay	delays	day	days	donkey	donkeys

Notes

◆ Most words add **s**.
◆ Add **es** if the word ends in a hissing/buzzing/shushing sound. Another way to remember this is to add **es** if you can hear an extra syllable when you make it plural. (The **e** is added to make the plural easier on the tongue, putting a buffer between too many **s** sounds.)
◆ Words ending in **e** – just add **s**.
◆ Words ending in **y** – add **s** if the final letter is preceded by a vowel. If not, change the **y** to **i** and add **es**.

Year 3
Term 2

Objective 10

To investigate, spell and read words with silent letters, e.g. *knee, gnat, wrinkle*

Whole-class approaches

◆ Read a specially prepared text pronouncing all silent letters. Ask the children to notice and then comment on the silent letters. Can they see patterns or do they know other examples?
◆ Place Post-It notes over the silent letters. Ask children to guess the silent letter underneath. Alternatively, write on the board a random list with silent letters deleted, and invite children to insert the letter.
◆ Investigation – list words on boards and ask children if they can see any common patterns (e.g. silent **k** at the beginning is always followed by **n**, and the **n** is always followed by a vowel).
◆ Make flashcards for **gn** and **kn**. Call out examples from Lists 1 and 2 below and ask the children to hold up the appropriate silent-letter card.

Group tasks

◆ Provide a set of cards in which the silent letter(s) have been separated from the rest of the word. Children match up letters with cards.
◆ Make collections of silent-letter words and work out patterns for different letters.
◆ Play Kim's game – children turn over two cards and keep any pair that has the same silent letters if they can pronounce the word.

List 1	List 2	List 3	List 4	List 5	List 6
knuckle	gnomes	write	rhyme	plumb	calf
knee	gnat	wrapper	rhubarb	dumb	half
knit	gnaw	wrong	wheat	numb	calm
knickers	gnu	wrist	whale	bomb	salmon
knob	gnash	wreck	when	tomb	chalk
knife	gnarled	wretch	whine	lamb	folk
knight		wrestle	rhino	thumb	yolk
knock		wrapper	honest	crumb	could
knot		wrinkle	chemist	debt	would
kneel		sword	whirl	doubt	should
know		answer			

Notes

◆ Silent **b** occurs after **m**, before **t**; silent **k** and silent **g** are found before **n**; silent **l** follows vowels **a**, **o** and **ou** – it produces a flat-sounding vowel; silent **w** often precedes **r**.
◆ The term 'silent letter' is perhaps misleading because **kn** is a digraph representing one phoneme in the same way that **th** or **es** do. Interestingly, however, most of the examples above have at some time in history been pronounced out loud, and have been silenced by fashion and language evolution. Changing pronunciation accounts for many unexpected aspects of the English spelling system.

Year 3 Term 2

Objective 12

To recognise and generate compound words, e.g. *playground, airport, shoelace, underneath;* and to use this knowledge to support their spelling

Whole-class approaches

◆ Display a selection of compound words. Invite children to spot what they have in common. Introduce the term *compound word*.
◆ Display the word *time*. Ask children to offer words that can be placed before or after *time* to make a list of compound words. Repeat using *green, day, eye* and *sand*.
◆ Use a page of a TV listings and invite children to take time out in pairs to identify as many programme names as they can which are compound words. Make a class list.

Group tasks

◆ Make a list of group addresses. Discuss and highlight any road names that combine two/three words to make a compound word.
◆ Use maps and atlases to collect place names that are compound words.
◆ Use an illustration of a Greek myth to spot objects that are compound words, e.g. *footpath, seaside, eyebrow*.
◆ Collect and categorise compound words, e.g. verbs/nouns/prepositions.
◆ Use cards containing common base words to create lists of compounds.

Useful base words		High-frequency words		Examples	Harder examples
sun	one	everyone	someone	churchyard	sideboard
time	woman	everybody	somebody	football	cupboard
man	no	everything	something	waistband	breakfast
play	any	nowhere	somewhere	paintbrush	deadline
mouth	some	no-one		upstairs	gunpowder
hand	where	nobody		bricklayer	windmill
day	thing	nothing		blackboard	bonfire
green	head	anywhere		weekend	dustbin
eye	every	anyone		earthworm	clockwise
sand	out	anybody		goalkeeper	grandmother
body	in	anything		playground	chambermaid

Notes

◆ Many compounds have historical roots to deduce or research (see final column).
◆ Compounds are two or three whole words that combine to make one.
◆ Compounds will most often be nouns.
◆ The spelling of the base words usually remains unchanged.

Year 3 Term 2

Objective 13

To recognise and spell common suffixes and how these influence word meanings, e.g. **ly**, **ful**, **less**

Whole-class approaches

◆ Create class collections of words with common suffixes and group them (e.g. see table below).
◆ Investigation – seek patterns, base words and generalisations about spellings, e.g. Why is 'islander' *island* + **er** but *voyager = voyag* + **er**? What do the suffixes mean?
◆ Create new words – fit base words to suffixes to create new words and define their meanings, e.g. *Oncer*.
◆ Draw together groups of words created by adding different suffixes to a base word, e.g. *careful, careless, carer, carefully*.

Group tasks

◆ Play a matching card game – matching the root word to its suffix.
◆ Use card wheel – root words on the front wheel and suffixes on the rear wheel. Real words can be identified and new words can be created.

ly	ful	less	er	able
kindly	wishful	careless	teacher	reliable
friendly	hopeful	thoughtless	reader	drinkable
properly	sorrowful	homeless	driver	touchable
actually	painful	lifeless	farmer	sinkable
especially	successful	fearless	Londoner	breakable
eventually	hateful	jobless	islander	enjoyable
originally	forgetful	thankless	villager	avoidable
personally	beautiful	headless	voyager	readable
weekly	resentful	speechless	manager	unavoidable
likely	pitiful	endless	teenager	arguable
really	merciful	merciless	baker	probable

Notes

◆ **ly**, **ful** and **less** are consonant suffixes. In most cases, the suffix is added without adaptation to the root word, except for words ending in **y**, which change to an **i**.
◆ **er** and **able** are vowel suffixes. If the root word ends in an **e** then it must be dropped before the suffix is added, e.g. *describe + able = describable*. If it ends in **y**, change the **y** to an **i**.
◆ **ly** means 'in this manner'.
◆ **ful** means 'full of'.
◆ **less** means 'without'.
◆ **er** means 'for' or 'belonging to'.
◆ **able** means 'able to'.

Year 3 Term 2

Objective 14

To use their knowledge of suffixes to generate new words from root words, e.g. *proud/proudly, hope/hopeful/hopeless*

Whole-class approaches

◆ Collect examples of words with suffixes, generalise about their effects on the base word, especially if it ends in **e** or **y**. Use the patterns to generate additional examples (real and invented) that belong in those groups.

◆ Brainstorm words with a particular suffix. Groups compete against the clock to collect most words.

◆ Use 'show me' cards – present a base word (see below) and ask children to brainstorm and show suitable suffixes.

Group tasks

◆ Find/invent synonyms for given words using the same suffix, e.g. *friendless/mateless; basinful/bowlful; fairly/justly*, and work out the meaning of the suffixes.

◆ Play 'Find the word' – from a given definition and a suffix find the right word, e.g. 'Which **ful** means "longing for something"?'

Some words as starting points for investigation

proud	like	sick	quiet	mind	glad
hope	kind	arm	room	thought	cold
nice	child	friend	doubt	sure	tune
home	care	fruit	life	lone	cheer
mist	time	hurt	rich	pain	shame
thirst	king	near	free	use	lone

Some useful suffixes

ship	ful	ness	ment	hood	less
er	est	ly	ish	dom	like

Notes

◆ The function of these suffixes is to change one part of speech into another, e.g. a noun to an adjective (*friend/friendly*).

◆ In some cases the root word needs modification before the suffix can be added, e.g. words ending in **y** and **e**.

Year 3 Term 2

To use the apostrophe to spell shortened forms of words, e.g. *don't, can't*

Whole-class approaches

◆ Display or write newspaper headlines which feature contraction apostrophes. Highlight the apostrophes. Teach the use of the apostrophe. Invite children to try placing apostrophes in words already contracted, but with the apostrophe removed. Emphasise that the apostrophe represents missing letters and not the joining of the two words.

◆ List the full forms. Invite the children to contract. Also try this vice versa – offer the contraction and invite children to expand.

◆ Use magnetic letters to demonstrate the replacement of letters with an apostrophe. Alternatively, use children holding whiteboard letters.

◆ Generalise about the type of words that attract contractions (verbs and pronouns).

Group tasks

◆ Check own written work.

◆ Word hunts.

◆ Discuss why a writer might choose an apostrophised form rather than the full form.

do not	don't	I had	I'd	she is/has	she's
cannot	can't	I would	I'd	he is/has	he's
is not	isn't	I have	I've	it is/has	it's
does not	doesn't	I will	I'll	there is/has	there's
will not	won't	I am	I'm		

Notes

◆ The contractions in this list are drawn from the high-frequency word lists.

◆ Apostrophes are used where two words have been joined and some letters missed out so that a contraction is formed.

◆ Note the homophone issue (*its/it's, there's/theirs*).

◆ Contractions occur more frequently in informal language.

Year 3
Term 3

Objective 8

Identify short words within longer words as an aid to spelling

Whole-class approaches

◆ Show a word on a magnetic board/class board. Ask the children to identify other words within it – the letters of these words must appear consecutively within the word on display.
◆ Focus on high-frequency words and invite suggestions for illustrating them to make the words memorable.

Group tasks

◆ Which of the children's names has the most words in it?
◆ Make a collection of subject-specific words which have other words within them, e.g. topic words, PE words. Give the collection to another group and challenge them to find the same (or a greater) number of words within words.
◆ Find a word with seven words within it. Which was the shortest word which had seven other words within it?
◆ Survey which are the most commonly occurring words within words.

Another	Something	Whatever	Father
a	so	what	fat
an	some	hat	at
no	me	hate	the
not	met	at	her
other	thin	ate	
the	in	eve	
he	thing	ever	
her			

Mother	Pretending	Constable	High-frequency words
moth	ten	con	that
other	tend	on	them
the	end	stable	then
he	ending	table	when
her	tending	stab	want
	din	tab	what
	in	able	where
			your
			friend

Notes

◆ Recognising words within words develops visual spelling strategies. It is important therefore that the words discovered have their letters appearing consecutively in the original word.
◆ Sometimes the words within words are roots which preserve their original meaning, e.g. *grand* + *mother*. Sometimes they are incidental.

Year 3 Term 3

To recognise and spell the prefixes **mis**, **non**, **ex**, **co**, **anti**

Whole-class approaches

◆ Display a list of words beginning with these prefixes and teach their meaning directly (see *Notes*).
◆ Look out for words in shared texts which have any of these prefixes. Cover with Post-It notes and ask children to work out the relevant prefix.
◆ Play Prefix Charades.
◆ Use Prefix Fans – teacher provides the root word and children select and show a suitable prefix.

Group tasks

◆ Children scan real texts – e.g. adverts, newspapers – and highlight prefix words with these prefixes.
◆ In pairs, children select and test each other on the spelling and meaning of words listed.

Extension activity

◆ Produce a 'new' list of words to promote an imaginary product, e.g. *anti-burglar, anti-frizz*! Create an advertisement for a product.

mis	non	ex	co	anti
misbehave	non-stick	exit	co-education	antidote
miscalculate	non-stop	extend	coincidence	antibiotic
misplace	non-smoker	explode	co-operate	antifreeze
miscount	non-violent	excursion	co-star	antiseptic
misdeal	non-starter	exchange	co-writer	anti-clockwise
misfire	nonsense	export		
misfortune	non-fiction	exclaim		
mishear	non-drip	external		
misinform		expel		
misread		exterior		
mistake		exile		

Notes

◆ **mis** means 'wrong', 'false'; **non** means 'not', 'opposite of'; **ex** means 'out' or 'outside of'; **co** means 'joint', 'together'; **anti** means 'against'; **col/l**, **comm**, **corr** are based on **co** and have the same meaning.
◆ New hyphenated words are appearing all the time, especially in advertising.

Year 3
Term 3

Objective 10

To use their knowledge of these prefixes to generate new words from root words, e.g. *lead/mislead, sense/nonsense,* and to understand how they give clues to meaning, e.g. *extend, export, explode; mislead, mistake, misplace*

Whole-class approaches

◆ Revise prefixes covered already – ask for two examples for every prefix.
◆ Revise by matching up sets of 'prefix' cards and 'meaning' cards.
◆ Write down ten words from the list of root words below, and ask them to experiment orally, making new words by adding different prefixes. Do they sound correct? Which words are more likely to be correct? How do we know? How can we check?

Group task

◆ Match prefix cards, as above, but using unfamiliar prefixes. Invite children to match them up by working out their meanings from known words.

Extension activity

◆ Thesaurus work
   – look up *beautiful* – list synonyms and experiment with adding prefixes;
   – make a list of 'bad behaviour' words and present at plenary – *unhelpful, antisocial, misbehaviour.*

Prefixes and meanings		More prefixes and meanings		Roots to work with	
re	again	pre	before	cool	sleep
de	undo	non	not	face	awaken
anti	against	inter	between	make	act
bi	two	ex	out of	dead	live
contra	against	un	not	grow	marine
in	not	sub	under	place	visit
ab	away from	mis	wrong	clean	write

Notes

◆ Remembering prefixes and their meanings helps both spelling and vocabulary.

Year 3
Term 3

Objective 11

To use the apostrophe to spell further contracted forms of words, e.g. *couldn't*

Whole-class approaches

◆ Remind the class of previous work on contractions. Display or write newspaper headlines which feature apostrophes for contractions from the word bank. Highlight the apostrophes. Invite the children to offer the extended forms and identify the missing letters. Emphasise that the apostrophe represents missing letters and not the joining of two words.
◆ Use magnetic letters to demonstrate the replacement of letters with an apostrophe. Alternatively, children could use individual whiteboards to attempt contractions.

Group tasks

◆ Word hunt and classify according to word contracted, e.g. *not, is, are, have, had, would, us* (*let's*).
◆ Using selected newspaper headlines, invite groups to discuss what the apostrophe represents and write in the missing letters above. Also discuss the reason for choosing the apostrophised form.
◆ Write two paragraphs describing a robbery – one a formal police report; the other by the victim. Why choose apostrophes?
◆ Use some of the words in the last column of the table below to generate discussion and find further examples of poetic licence, dialect and word play.

Pronouns				Other contractions	
I'm	I'll	I've	I'd	can't	o'clock
You're	You'll	You've	You'd	won't	'tis
He's	He'll	He's	He'd	shan't	ma'am
She's	She'll	She's	She'd	aren't	mix 'n' match
We're	We'll	We've	We'd	hadn't	Toys 'Я' Us
They're	They'll	They've	They'd	haven't	salt 'n' vinegar
				couldn't	pick 'n' mix
				weren't	tell 'em

Notes

◆ Apostrophes are used where two or more words have been joined and some letters missed out so that a contraction is formed.
◆ Contractions occur more frequently in informal language.
◆ *Won't* and *shan't* are unusual because the base words have been modified.
◆ In older texts, *would, should* and *could* are shortened using *'ld*.

Year 3
Term 3

Objective 14

To explore homonyms which have the same spelling but multiple meanings and explain how the meanings can be distinguished in context, e.g. *form* (shape or document), *wave* (gesture, shape or motion)

Whole-class approaches

◆ From a collection of mixed words, invite the children to spot any that have two meanings. Teach the term *homonym*.
◆ Display pairs of sentences which use the same homonyms. Ask the children to read them aloud. Discuss how they worked out which image to bring to mind. Emphasise the significance of context and meaning.
◆ Show sets of five words – each set contains one word which is not a homonym. Play Spot the Odd One Out.
◆ Show a joke where word play has used homonyms. Discuss how humour was created.
◆ Display pairs of sentences that use words from the list below which have the same spelling but different meaning **and** pronunciation. Ask children to read aloud. How did they know which pronunciation to use? Emphasise the importance of context to make sense.

Group tasks

◆ Make sets of 'odd one out' for other groups to guess.
◆ Search for funny poems, jokes and puns. Explain how they work.
◆ Compose pairs of sentences using homonyms, e.g. *Mum gave her son a wave. Sam jumped over the wave.* Illustrate humorous absurdities, e.g. Sam jumping over his mother's waving hand.

Homonyms					Contrasting sounds
age	crane	letter	leaves	watch	bow
fit	club	spot	flat	dear	tear
train	bank	grate	table	jam	row
fat	light	snap	safe	arms	wind
rose	pop	warm	plain	wave	lead
form	tug	lead	plane	last	wound
ring	stand	race	float	bat	sow
sound	book	gum	foot	yard	read

Notes

◆ Homonyms lend themselves to the discussion of grammar, e.g. their relationship to other words in a sentence shows whether they are a verb, a noun or an adjective.

Year 4
Term 1

To spell two-syllable words containing double consonants, e.g. *bubble, kettle, common*

Year 4 Objectives

Whole-class approaches
◆ Warm up with oral activities distinguishing between long and short (rap) vowels.
◆ Use the contrasting words list to show how long vowels in the middle of words are followed by one consonant, but short vowels are followed by two.
◆ Distribute prepared cards among the children and ask each child in turn to read aloud their word. Ask the rest to work out whether it has a long or short sound, and therefore one or two consonants. The child holds up their card to show the right answer.
◆ Use whiteboards so that children can attempt simple words applying this rule.

Group tasks
◆ Make lists of family or topic words with double letters after short vowels (see below).
◆ Learn the high-frequency words (see below).

Extension activities
◆ Create a double-letter alphabet, e.g. *rabbit, sudden, scuffle*.
◆ Work out which consonants never make doubles and why not.
◆ What happens in words of more than two syllables?
◆ Exceptions: **mod** words (*modern, modest, model*, etc.)

Contrasting words					
diner	dinner	writing	written	hoping	hopping
biter	bitter	taping	tapping	super	supper
coma	comma	pole	pollen	lady	laddy

Thematic words					
Adjectives	happy	messy	silly	jolly	funny
Animals	rabbit	puppy	kitten	otter	hippo
Verbs	grabbed	messed	kissed	bossed	fussed
Cooking	batter	butter	pepper	carrot	coffee
Garden	apple	willow	holly	cherry	berry

High-frequency words					
common	rotten	letter	tennis	better	happy
follow	sudden	stopped	swimming	penny	mummy
daddy	puppy	dinner	shopping	getting	silly
pillow	swallow	carry	summer	butter	cotton
funny	running	happy	sorry	written	kettle

Notes
◆ Double the letter after a short (rap) vowel in the middle of words.
◆ No words use **hh, jj, kk, qq, vv, ww, xx**.
◆ Some imported words use **cc** (*broccoli, cappuccino*).

Year 4
Term 1

Objective 6

To distinguish between the spelling and meanings of common homophones, e.g. *to/two/too; they're/their/there; piece/peace*

Whole-class approaches

◆ Teach words and meanings directly, and display.
◆ Place Post-It notes over homophones in shared texts and ask children to work out which one fits.
◆ Make individual flashcards (e.g. *there/their*) for children and ask them to hold up the correct spelling in response to a sentence in which the meaning is clear.
◆ Riddles – 'What opens locks and is always found beside water?'

Group tasks

◆ Play Kim's game – place cards face-down and hunt out the pairs. You can claim a pair if you can prove you know the correct meaning using a dictionary.
◆ Play Sound Snap with a limited number of priority words.
◆ Invent mnemonics and ways of working out the correct choice.
◆ Play Beat the Spellchecker – write a 100-word story or report that beats the spellchecker. Team with the most cheats wins.

Extension activities

◆ Look for homonyms (same spelling, different meanings, e.g. *bear*).
◆ Research history of words to explain the origin of some homophones' spellings.

were	where	we're	you	yew	ewe
their	they're	there	too	two	to

be	bee	see	sea	heard	herd
new	knew	no	know	might	mite
right	write	morning	mourning	place	plaice
through	threw	great	grate	eyes	ice
hole	whole	I	eye	for	four
are	our	in	inn	of	have

Notes

◆ The homophones in this list apply to the high frequency word list only. For further homophones, consult Y5.T2.O6.
◆ Many homophone choices are best taught as a grammatical issue, e.g. *there/their*.
◆ Analogy with family groups can be helpful, e.g. *our, your; here, where, there*.

Year 4 Term 1

Objective 7

To spell regular verb endings **s**, **ed**, **ing** (link to grammar work on tenses)

Whole-class approaches

◆ Investigate how each ending is added in each of the four cases listed below. Use lists to encourage children to generalise and add further examples.
◆ Whiteboard activity – children write correct form in response to a spoken word.
◆ Play human spellings. Distribute large letter cards (or create using individual whiteboards), including plenty of **y**, **i**, **e** and **s** cards. Invite children to group together to create a verb ending in **y**, then ask the **i**, **e** and **y** children to form a 3rd person singular form.

Group tasks

◆ Play card sorts, matches and games, e.g. collect word families, collect **es** endings.
◆ Use a selection of words on the list to make word sums for the children, e.g. *drop* + **ed** = _____, *save* + **ing** = _____, *wash* + **s** = _____
◆ Make concertina books which incorporate a time line. Children record personal experience or historical knowledge using words on the list, e.g. *When I was three I look**ed** like this ... Now I look like this .... The Tudors travell**ed** by horse .... In the future we'll all be travell**ing** in electric cars.* Use writing frames to help less confident children.
◆ Use the lists below for word investigations, e.g. can children spot the rule for doubling of consonants? Can they find further examples of the word families on the lists below?

Typical of most words			Ending in consonant + y		
cooks	cooked	cooking	carries	carried	carrying
plays	played	playing	cries	cried	crying
invents	invented	inventing	marries	married	marrying
jumps	jumped	jumping	relies	relied	relying
looks	looked	looking	spies	spied	spying
shows	showed	showing	tries	tried	trying
works	worked	working	fries	fried	frying
Short vowels			**Ending in hissing/buzzing sounds**		
drags	dragged	dragging	touches	touched	touching
drops	dropped	dropping	washes	washed	washing
grabs	grabbed	grabbing	buzzes	buzzed	buzzing
hugs	hugged	hugging	hisses	hissed	hissing
shops	shopped	shopping	rushes	rushed	rushing
stops	stopped	stopping	fixes	fixed	fixing
Ending in e			fizzes	fizzed	fizzing
saves	saved	saving	wishes	wished	wishing
notes	noted	noting			
explores	explored	exploring			

Notes

◆ It is difficult to practise the future tense, not least because the future tense does not exist as such in English, but is formed in combination with other verbs (I will go, I am going to go).
◆ Most verbs simply add **s**, **ed** and **ing** to indicate tenses.
◆ When a single-syllable verb ends with a consonant preceded by a short vowel you double the final consonant when adding **ed** or **ing**.
◆ If a word ends in **e**, avoid the double **e** by dropping one as necessary.
◆ If a word ends in a consonant plus **y**, change **y** to **i** before adding **es** or **ed**, but to avoid creating a double **i**, keep the **y** in place for the adding of **ing**.
◆ If a word ends in a hissing or buzzing sound, add an **e** before the **s**. This makes it sayable, and helpfully creates an extra syllable.

23

Year 4 Term 1

Objective 8

To spell irregular tense changes, e.g. *go/went, can/could*

Whole-class approaches

◆ Establish conventional tense endings, e.g. **ed**. Brainstorm or collect up irregular tense endings and sort them into like groups, e.g. **ow – ew**; **ing – ang**; **ind – ound**; **ell – old**.

◆ Reinforce the past/present concept by using adverbials (*Last year ... Long ago ... Today ... Now*).

◆ Create poems and texts in Shared Writing that draw on tense transformations, e.g. *Then/Now – Once we **ate** food that was mushy and gooey. Now we **eat** burgers and chips and chop suey.*

Group tasks

◆ Make small books entitled *A History of Me*. Left-hand pages record past experiences. Right-hand pages record present experiences. Use writing frames to help less confident children use words on the list.

◆ Play card sorts, matches and games (e.g. Rummy) using pairs from the list below. Cut cards into onsets and rimes to play word dominoes to make it more challenging.

blow	blew	think	thought	eat	ate
grow	grew	fight	fought	can	could
throw	threw	buy	bought	go	went
know	knew	take	took	is	was
sing	sang	shake	shook	are	were
ring	rang	wear	wore	have	had
drink	drank	tear	tore	does	did
begin	began	tell	told	get	got
feed	fed	sell	sold	hear	heard
meet	met	rise	rose	make	made
creep	crept	write	wrote	sit	sat
keep	kept	ride	rode	shoot	shot
sleep	slept	drive	drove	teach	taught
sweep	swept	speak	spoke	catch	caught
weep	wept	break	broke	bite	bit
find	found	give	gave	hide	hid
wind	wound	see	saw	send	sent
swim	swam	dig	dug	spend	spent
run	ran	slide	slid	bend	bent

Notes

◆ These irregular plural forms are survivals from Old English in which change of medial vowel was widely used to indicate change of tense. They are called 'strong' verbs in some textbooks.

Year 4
Term 1

Objective 9 (1 of 2)

To recognise and spell the suffixes **al**, **ary**, **ic**

Whole-class approaches
◆ In Shared Reading and Writing identify words with these suffixes (use the term *suffix*) and, over a period of weeks, build lists of these words.
◆ Investigation – what is the general meaning of the suffixes and what spelling patterns do they follow?

Group tasks
◆ Investigation – using dictionaries, including rhyming and crossword dictionaries, collect words to add to the class collections of words with one or other of these suffixes.
◆ Investigation – identify the root words behind some words with these suffixes.

al		ary		ic	
medical	traditional	stationary	February	historic	organic
personal	capital	dictionary	salary	supersonic	atomic
seasonal	vocal	revolutionary		specific	traffic
exceptional		missionary		horrific	
occasional		necessary		metallic	
national		anniversary		angelic	
sensational		library		epidemic	
additional				rhythmic	

Notes
◆ **al**, **ary** and **ic** are vowel suffixes. Root words drop a final **e** or change **y** to **i** before taking the suffix.
◆ **al** often follows **on** and **ic**.
◆ **ary** – in some cases the root is not always obvious, e.g. *temporary* = *tempor(al)* + **ary**. Unstressed, it is often confused with **ery**. One approach is to seek out base words ending in **e** to indicate **ery**, e.g. *stationer* or *saddle*.
◆ Roots are often hard to detect in this group of words.

Year 4
Term 1

To recognise and spell the suffixes **ship**, **hood**, **ness**, **ment**

Whole-class approaches

◆ In Shared Reading and Writing identify words with these suffixes (use the term *suffix*) and, over a period of weeks, build lists of these words.
◆ Investigation – what is the general meaning of the suffixes, e.g. what does **ship** mean in *ownership, authorship*, etc?

Group tasks

◆ Investigation – using dictionaries, including rhyming and crossword dictionaries, collect words to add to the class collections of words with one or other of these suffixes.
◆ Investigation – identify the root words behind some words with these suffixes.
◆ Investigation of similar suffixes, e.g. **dom, like, ish, some, ance, ence, ism, ology, craft, ation.**
◆ Investigation of multiple suffixes, e.g. *worthlessness*.

ship	hood	ness	ment
membership	childhood	fairness	enjoyment
ownership	falsehood	kindness	employment
partnership	priesthood	tidiness	ornament
dictatorship	neighbourhood	loveliness	document
workmanship	fatherhood	silliness	management
championship	motherhood	nastiness	environment
craftsmanship	knighthood	wickedness	government
apprenticeship		childishness	replacement
fellowship		willingness	ointment
		fitness	statement
		worthlessness	movement
		carelessness	
		foolishness	
		left-handedness	
		absent-mindedness	

Notes

◆ **ship**, **hood**, **ness** and **ment** are simply added unless a final **y** needs to be changed to **i**.
◆ Roots are often hard to detect in this group of words.
◆ The language is full of suffixes which suggest a state of being.

Year 4 Term 1

Objective 14

The ways in which nouns and adjectives. e.g. *fix, simple, solid, drama, dead* can be made into verbs by use of the suffixes **ate**, **ify**, etc.; investigate spelling patterns and generate rules to govern the patterns

Whole-class approaches

◆ Make a verb factory – build lists of words over time by brainstorming or collecting from shared text, to show how nouns, adjectives and verbs can be formed from each other.
◆ Investigation – collect and generalise about the way words attach suffixes to change their function. Establish patterns and rules.

Group tasks

◆ Play word-match games – match verb card to its adjective or noun.
◆ Play Make a Verb game – invent new verbs from nouns/adjectives, e.g. *nice/nicify* (not so far-fetched – think of *pretty* and *prettify*).
◆ Word sort – put words into two piles: those that will have to undergo a change before adding a verb suffix and those that won't.
◆ Investigate exceptions when creating nouns, e.g. *poor – poverty; clear – clarity; curious – curiosity*.

Into verbs (ate, en, ify, ise)		Into nouns (tion, ity, ness)		Useful base words for activities	
pollen	pollinate	educate	education	clear	fertile
note	notify	dictate	dictation	deaf	light
elastic	elasticate	create	creation	solid	straight
medicine	medicate	simple	simplicity	quantity	glory
apology	apologise	able	ability	category	good
standard	standardise	pure	purity	loose	like
length	lengthen	stupid	stupidity	dark	flat
deep	deepen	hard	hardness	appetite	horror
dead	deaden	happy	happiness	class	poor
pure	purify	mad	madness	less	mobile

Notes

◆ One of the functions of a suffix is to change a part of speech; in this case a noun or an adjective into a verb and a verb or adjective into a noun.
◆ The main suffixes are listed above; others are: **efy** (*liquefy*) and **esce** (*effervesce*).
◆ Most words just add the suffix.
◆ When the root word already has a suffix, or it ends in **e** or **y**, it has to be removed before the new suffix can be added. Watch out, however, for words ending in **y** if you are adding **ness** – the **y** changes to **i**. Fortunately, the **i** is clearly pronounced.

Year 4
Term 2

Objective 5

To investigate what happens to words ending in **f** when suffixes are added

Whole-class approaches

◆ Investigation – collect up words ending in **f** and **fe** and their plurals. Generalise the spelling rules.
◆ Use 'show me' cards for **fs** and **ves**.
◆ In Shared Reading or oral storytelling, cover endings with Post-It notes and ask children to work out the correct endings. (*A Visit to the Zoo* would naturally include several of the target words.)
Alternative: Teacher models story using the singular forms in column 1, then tells the story using plural forms. Children hold up correct cards for endings used.

Group tasks

◆ Play Kim's game (in pairs) with flashcards.
◆ Use *Where's Wally?* books by Martin Handford to make a game, or display identifying target words in the pictures.

F/ves		ff/s		Words ending in **e**	
calf	calves	cuff	cuffs	knife	knives
elf	elves	staff	staffs	life	lives
half	halves	sniff	sniffs	safe	saves
leaf	leaves	puff	puffs	wife	wives
loaf	loaves	stuff	stuffs	believe	believes
self	selves	cliff	cliffs	glove	gloves
scarf	scarves	bluff	bluffs	curve	curves
self	selves			swerve	swerves
shelf	shelves				
thief	thieves			**Unusual words**	
wolf	wolves			belief	beliefs
				chief	chiefs

Notes

◆ Most words ending in **f** change to **ves** in the plural.
◆ Words ending in **ff** add **s**.
◆ Words ending in **fe** use **ves**.
◆ Sometimes a **ves** ending indicates a change of word class from noun to verb, e.g. *belief – believes*; *grief – grieves*; *proof – proves*.

Year 4 Term 2

Objective 6

To spell words with the common endings: **ight**, etc.

Whole-class approach

◆ Build lists of words with common endings. Investigate for patterns, e.g parts of speech. Identify spelling difficulties (e.g. phonological variety of **ough**) and model strategies for problem-solving (see *Notes* below).

Group tasks

◆ Use crossword/rhyming dictionaries to build lists of words with common endings.
◆ Using lists of words with a common ending look for patterns, e.g. part of speech, syllable counts, etc.
◆ Look for mnemonics or other tricks to fix the spelling of tricky words.

ight	tion	ious	ial	ough
light	reaction	infectious	partial	bough
fight	subtraction	previous	special	although
night	electrocution	obvious	official	through
right	promotion	tedious	racial	cough
bright	devotion	serious	artificial	rough
slight	composition	glorious	financial	tough
fright	ambition	curious	social	enough

Notes

◆ **ight** – most words ending in the 'ight' sound use **ight**. A handful of words use the split digraph **i-e** (but they include common words like *white, kite*). A number of scientific terms end in **ite**, (e.g. *bauxite*) or **yte** (e.g. *byte*). **ight** words are generally nouns.
◆ **tion** – words ending in **tion** are almost exclusively nouns. The **tion** ending is generally predictable from its sound. Exceptions can generally be sorted out: adjectives (chiefly to do with nationality) often end in **ian** (e.g. *Russian*); nouns of occupation often end in **cian** (e.g. optician) and there is a tiny handful of isolates (e.g. *ocean*). See Y5 T2 O8 for further detail and ideas to stretch able children.
◆ **ious** – the **ious** ending is generally predictable from its sound, and there are relatively few exceptions (*hideous, beauteous, plenteous*). **ious** words are generally adjectives.
◆ **ial** – the **ial** ending is almost entirely stable, and preceded by either **t** or **c**. There are relatively few exceptions. **ial** words are generally adjectives.
◆ **ough** – an example of extreme variation. Best learnt by exception: *bough, plough* (and perhaps *Slough*, the town) are effectively the only occasions when the final 'ow' sound is made by **ough** rather than by **ow**. *Through* is an isolate – the only case of an 'oo' sound. *Though, dough, thought* and *thorough* are also isolates. That leaves words like *tough* and *enough*, which are also isolates (other words use **uff**).

Year 4 Term 2

Objective 7

To recognise and spell the prefixes: **al**, etc.

Whole-class approaches

◆ Display lists of words (see table below), and teach the meanings of the prefixes, thus teasing out the meanings of the words.
◆ Display cards with prefixes and roots and ask children to join up and define words which use both.

Group task

◆ Ask groups to devise a 100-word story using the **a** words linked by meaning. Suitable titles include *Sea-Saga*, *Battle* or *Summer Garden*.

Extension activities

◆ Ask children to look for older poetry which may use words like *abloom*, *aglitter*.
◆ Skim through a dictionary, looking for new words to add to the lists below – these must hold to the meaning of the prefix.

ad	af	al	a		
adjective	affix	almighty	aloft	another	asleep
adverb	affable	alone	aground	abide	awake
admire	affection	almost	afield	aglitter	alive
advance	affect	already	aboard	abloom	alert
advise	affluent	always	away	afloat	ablaze
advent	afflict	altogether	astride	around	apart
addition	affirm	also			
adjoin		although			
adjacent					
adjust					

Notes

◆ **ad** means 'towards' – just add; **af** means 'tending towards' – double the **f**; **al** means 'all' + base word – drop one of the **l**s; **a** means 'in a state of' (words in the **a** list above have a sense of 'on' or 'in') – just add.
◆ Teach words within words, e.g. **an** + *other* = *another*.

Year 4
Term 3

Objective 5 (1 of 2)

To explore the occurrence of certain letters within words, e.g. **v** and **k**; deduce some of the conventions for using them at the beginnings, middles and endings of words

Whole-class approach
◆ Brainstorm examples in three columns – beginning, middle, end. Review differences in sound.

Group task
◆ Provide word cards using **v** and **k** and ask children to categorise by sound, then work out where it appears in a word most frequently, and what letters commonly precede or follow it.

Extension activity
◆ Draw up a new grid for other letters. Interesting examples include: **h**, **c**, **p**, **g**, **q**, **t**, **x**, **y**.

v			k		
Beginning	**Middle**	**End**	**Beginning**	**Middle**	**End**
van	river	none	kick	broken	back
vase	novel		kill	shaken	dock
value	saved		keen	taken	kick
valley	wives		keep	tickle	trick
variety	caves		kept	pickle	work
vegetable	diver		kennel	choking	pork
verb	favour		kettle	stoked	tank
vein	given		kestrel	token	sink
veal	hover		kiss	crackle	wink
village	prevent		kit	stricken	walk
visit	liver		king	chuckle	talk
visa	savage		kerb	wrinkle	milk
visible	invent		kitten	ankle	lurk

Notes
◆ **v** – no words end in **v**, except colloquials, e.g. *gov, spiv*.
◆ **k** – often preceded by **l**, **r**, **n** and **c** at the ends of words – *wok* and *yak* are exceptional because the **k** is preceded by a vowel.

Year 4
Term 3

Objective 5 (2 of 2)

To explore the occurrence of certain letter strings, e.g. **wa** (e.g. *swat, water*), **wo** (e.g. *worship, won*) and **ss** (e.g. *goodness, hiss, missile*) within words; deduce some of the conventions for using them at the beginnings, middles and endings of words

Whole-class approach

◆ Brainstorm examples in three columns – beginning, middle, end. Review differences in sound.

Group task

◆ Provide word cards using the same letter string and ask children to categorise by sound, then work out where it appears in a word most frequently, and what letters commonly precede or follow it.

Extension activity

◆ Draw up a new grid for other letter combinations, e.g. **oo**, **ch**, **sc**, which change their sounds in different contexts.

wa		wo		ss	
Beginning	**Middle**	**Beginning**	**Middle**	**Beginning**	**End**
was	swamp	woman	swollen	*none*	guess
wasp	swallow	wok	sword		process
wander	dwarf	women	swore	**Middle**	goodness
war	swat	won't	awoke	session	likeness
wag	swarm	would		massive	fuss
warn	reward	wolf	**End**	lesson	discuss
want	swan	worry	two	possible	less
wait	towards	woof		missile	possess
wage	beware	wound		discussion	helpless
wake		wonder		passion	boss
wave	**End**	work		Russian	hiss
wash	*none*	wobble		procession	miss
watch		woke		possession	kiss
wax		wool			assess
water		word			success
wallet		worm			pass

Notes

◆ **wa** – often makes a long flat 'a' sound. Short **a** is uncommon. **swa** is a common string. No examples at the ends of words.
◆ **wo** – vast majority of examples with **wo** at the beginning; *two* is the only example with **wo** ending. **swo** is about the only string which places it in the middle of words unless you count compound words such as *waxworks* or *roadworthy*.
◆ **ss** – common at the end of words because of the **ness** and **less** suffixes, but note it changes to a 'sh' sound when you add an **ion** or **ian** ending, e.g. *discuss/discussion*. No words begin with **ss**.

Year 4 Term 3

To spell words with common letter strings but different pronunciations, e.g. *tough, through, trough, plough; hour, journey, could, route, four*

Whole-class approaches

◆ Make class lists of words that exhibit common letter strings but are pronounced differently. Make connections to words that follow the same pattern (e.g. *near* and *hear; bear* and *wear*).

◆ Identify overlaps (e.g. *clear* and *pier*) and discuss and generate strategies for avoiding confusion (e.g. 'I measured the h<u>eight</u> and w<u>eight</u> of <u>eight</u> people'.)

Group tasks

◆ Use crossword dictionaries and other resources to create lists of words with common letter strings but different pronunciations. Try **ough**, **ow**, **ai**, **ry**, **ie**, **gh**.

◆ Investigation– identify patterns:
  ◆ Which pronunciation is the most common?
  ◆ Which pronunciation is least common?
  ◆ Do pronunciations follow any patterns? (Try looking at position in word, letters preceding and letters following.)

◆ Identify mnemonics and other tricks to avoid potential confusions (e.g. *tough* and *stuff*).

ough	ear	ight	ou	au	ice
tough	bear	light	out	aunt	practice
rough	hear	might	shout	sausage	notice
enough	wear	right	hour	haunt	police
cough	learn	bright	pour	autumn	nice
trough	earn	sight	yours	aura	spice
plough	hearth	tight	would	Laura	twice
thought	dear	weight	mourn	sauce	mice
though	dreary	freight	four	pause	rice
thorough	weary	height	route	cause	dice
through	fear	fight	journey	because	apprentice
	gear	night	could	trauma	Alice

Notes

◆ Note that accent and dialect have an impact on how words are pronounced in a locality.

◆ A feature of our sound-spelling system is that the same letter string can often be used to code more than one phoneme. In some cases the number of words involved is so small that they can be learned almost as isolates, e.g. there are only five words that end in **eight**. The most common sound is shared by *eight, weight* and *freight*; the other two words are *height* and *sleight*. Even the groups which are more numerous are within reasonable limits. For example, the group showing the greatest variety in the table above is *tough, through, trough, plough* and *thought*. Investigation will show that the number of <u>common</u> words that follow those models is quite small:

  tough – two cases (*tough, rough*);
  through – one case;
  trough – two cases (*trough, cough*);
  plough – two cases (*bough, plough*);
  thought – four cases (*bought, thought, nought, sought*).

Year 4
Term 3

Objective 7

Collect/classify words with common roots, e.g. *advent, invent, prevent, press, pressure, depress, phone, telephone, microphone*; investigate origins and meanings

Whole-class approaches
◆ Provide and explain a root, then brainstorm and explain examples of it in use.
◆ Provide a list of words using the same root, and ask children to deduce the meaning.
◆ In Shared Reading, identify words built around common roots.
◆ Create word webs showing words related to a common root.
◆ Invent new words by combining common roots and affixes.

Group tasks
◆ Use dictionaries and other word lists to create collections of words with common roots. (A rhyming dictionary will help to uncover words where the common root is at the end.)
◆ Use an etymological dictionary to create charts showing word links and origins.

Words derived from other languages

from *dec* – ten	from *annus* – year	from *manus* – hand
decad	annual	manual
decimal	anniversary	manuscript
from *graphein* – write	from *aqua* – water	from *mort* – dead
graph	aquarium	mortgage
photograph	aqueduct	mortuary
from *mikros* – small	from *unus* – one	from *roi* – king
microscope	unit	royal
microlight	union	royalty
from *octo* – eight	from *insula* – island	from *presse* – press
octagon	insulation	express
octopus	peninsula	pressure
from *skopein* – to see	from *nun* – name	from *voix* – voice
telescope	noun	voice
microscope	announce	vocal
from *ge* – earth	from *specere* – to look	from *bloc* – block
geology	spectator	blockage
geography	spectrum	blockade
from *naus* – ship	from *dictare* – to say	from *copie* – plenty
nausea	dictator	copy
nautical	dictionary	photocopy

Notes
◆ Many roots are derived from other languages, Greek, Latin and French in particular. Investigation of these roots can make plain commonalities in spelling which phonology sometimes obscures (e.g. the link between *reign* and *sovereign*).
◆ See later objectives for further examples to stretch the able and interested.

Year 4
Term 3

Objective 8

To practise extending and compounding words through adding parts, e.g. **ful**, **ly**, **ive**, **tion**, **ic**, **ist**; revise and investigate links between meaning and spelling

Whole-class approaches

◆ In Shared Writing, experiment with word extension, evaluating the impact of alternatives, e.g. *costly/expensive*.
◆ Investigation – identify base words from extended words, e.g. what is the base word behind *manic*?
◆ Build up words using multiple affixes, e.g. *thank + full +* **ly** *= thankfully*.
◆ Find words which use more than one suffix, e.g. *correct – correctly, corrective, correction*.

Group tasks

◆ Use word wheels – base words on the front wheel and suffixes behind. Children have to match the right suffix to the base word.
◆ Create new words by combining base words and suffixes, e.g. *computerist*.
◆ Investigation – infer rules from examining cases, e.g. why is it *hurtful* but not *beautyful*?

ful	ly	ive	tion	ic	ist
hopeful	quickly	explosive	correction	horrific	extremist
hurtful	secretively	corrosive	construction	photographic	machinist
wishful	thickly	expensive	production	terrific	violinist
beautiful	jokingly	relative	variation	allergic	artist
careful	strangely	narrative	resurrection	comic	balloonist
merciful	speedily	active	creation	energetic	instrumentalist
wonderful	normally	decorative	pollination	scientific	specialist
painful	wholly	furtive	examination	manic	novelist
thankful	curiously	massive	education	acidic	stockist

Notes

◆ **ful**, **ly** and **tion** are consonant suffixes. Generally, these consonant suffixes can be added without alteration to the base word, except for words ending in **y** which change to **i**. There are a few exceptions, e.g. *wholly*. Words ending in **t** drop the **t** before adding **tion**, e.g. *construction*. The underlying principle is to avoid an impossible glut of sounds in the mouth.
◆ **ive**, **ic** and **ist** are vowel suffixes. Before adding one of these vowel suffixes you must drop a final **e** or **y**.

Year 4 Term 3

Objective 9

To recognise and spell the suffixes: **ible**, **able**, **ive**, **tion**, **sion**

Whole-class approaches

◆ In Shared Reading and Writing, identify words with these suffixes and build class collections organised under common headings. See lists below.

◆ Investigation – identify the root words. What changes have been made to these roots before adding the suffix? What generalisations can be made about rules, e.g. 'What happens if the root word ends in **e**? Or in **y**? Why *touchable* but not *stopable*?'

◆ Use 'show me' suffix cards for **able** and **ible** to be shown in response to a word.

Group task

◆ Investigation – find words that can take more than one of these suffixes, e.g. *adorable/adoration; identifiable/identification; prevention/preventable*.

ible	able	ive	tion	sion
horrible	miserable	forgive	inflation	decision
terrible	probable	massive	vibration	division
responsible	adorable	excessive	dictation	supervision
possible	respectable	aggressive	temptation	explosion
edible	forgivable	decisive	education	corrosion
reversible	disposable	explosive	expectation	confusion
invincible	agreeable	exclusive	conservation	transfusion
indestructible	enviable	expensive	creation	television
susceptible	identifiable	native	variation	conclusion
	enjoyable	inquisitive	pronunciation	collision
	valuable	competitive	punctuation	extension
	breakable	motive	communication	
	reliable	relative	qualification	
		active	navigation	
		attractive		
		captive		
		deceptive		

Notes

◆ Final **e** deletion is common in the root word, e.g. *reversible, valuable, creation*.

◆ **able** endings are far more common than **ible** ones. A key to distinguishing between these endings is that dropping **able** leaves a generally recognisable word, e.g. *agreeable*; dropping **ible** usually leaves a stem, e.g. *legible*. If one can say 'I am able to…', then the word is usually **able**. **ible** usually follows words ending in **s**.

◆ **tion** words are far more common than **sion**, and are often preceded by an **a**.

◆ Many **sion** words are can be grouped together, e.g. *inclusion/conclusion/exclusion; infusion/transfusion/effusion/diffusion; illusion/delusion*. They are often formed from verbs ending in **d** or **de**, e.g. *decide, explode*.

Year 4
Term 3

Objective 10

To distinguish the two forms: *its* (possessive, no apostrophe) and *it's* (contracted 'it is') and to use these accurately in own writing

Whole-class approaches

◆ If possible, find a text with examples of both words. Discuss difference. Try covering examples with Post-It notes and ask children to work out the correct version.

◆ Work out ways of distinguishing the two, e.g. If you can substitute *it is*, then the correct form is *it's*. Another way might be to think of the apostrophe in *it's* as the top of the missing letter **i**.

◆ Use 'show me' cards containing *its* and *it's*. You provide sentences and they hold up the correct card. Alternatively, use individual whiteboards, and ask children to write *its* in large handwriting. They can write in or rub out the apostrophe as appropriate. Sample sentences:

Whose coat is this? _____ mine!
_____ a lovely day today.
The elephant raised _____ trunk.
Hurry up, _____ going to rain!
The monster opened _____ mouth and roared.
The book had lost _____ last page.

Group tasks

◆ Make *it's*/*its* into 'target words'. Make a reminder card with the rules for remembering which is which.

◆ Create a flow chart to test for which form to use.

◆ Cloze. Insert correct version in a text where they are plentiful, but deleted.

◆ Play pairs or snap with four sets of cards: *it is*, *it's*, *its*, *belonging to it*.

it's	its

Notes

◆ *It's* = it is;
◆ *its* = belonging to it.

Year 4
Term 3

To investigate compound words and recognise that they can aid spelling even where pronunciation obscures it, e.g. *handbag, cupboard*

Whole-class approaches
◆ Make class collections of compound words by brainstorming or by collecting over a period of time from shared texts, for example. Identify the original words and any letters that are obscured by pronunciation.
◆ Shuffle cards to create new compound words.

Group tasks
◆ Match words to form standard compounds or to create new ones.
◆ Develop definitions which show the difference in meaning between compound words and the word elements used on their own, e.g. what is the difference between a *grandmother* and a *grand mother*?
◆ Investigation – develop possible explanations for the change in pronunciation in some compound words, and what their origins might be, e.g. *cupboard – board* used to mean 'table'.
◆ Create highly visual A4 wall posters to 'advertise' the original components of compound words.

Easy compounds			Tricky and curious compounds		
windmill	weekend	everyone	cloakroom	cupboard	starboard
bedroom	outside	anybody	handkerchief	joystick	blackboard
football	blackbird	database	grandmother	popcorn	handbag
tablecloth	grasshopper	playground	goodnight	household	raspberry

A selection of base words					
in	to	house	wards	hold	grand
out	good	cloak	night	land	lord
box	school	dust	god	bin	child
farm	home	any	yard	work	one
back	bath	no	room	thing	ground
star	moon	shine	burst	pot	time
post	man	light	tea	wife	son
bed	some	play	stead	where	side

Notes
◆ A compound word is a word made up from two or more other words. A characteristic of compounds is that they are almost always pronounced with the stress on the first word element. Solid compounds are written as a single word, hyphenated compounds are linked with a hyphen, e.g. *leg-iron*. Over time, the meaning of compound words has drifted, adding an historical interest, e.g. *cloakroom* has survived the arrival of coats instead of cloaks. The days of the week and words like *blackguard* often yield to historical research. *Biscuit* means 'twice-baked' in French. Thus, some apparently unreasonable spellings can be explained.
◆ Most compounds work by simply adding the two base words together without modification. If the first word ends in **y**, that will often change to **i**, e.g. *handicraft*.

Year 4
Term 3

Objective 12

To understand how diminutives are formed, e.g. suffixes: **ette**; prefixes: **mini**; adjectives, e.g. *little*; nouns, e.g. *sapling*; and nicknames, e.g. *Jonesy*

Whole-class approaches

◆ In shared text time, identify adjectives which indicate smallness.
◆ Brainstorm using one key word from each list to start children off. Identify the affix that indicates smallness, and also the root, e.g. *cigar* + **ette**.
◆ Discuss why diminutives are used, e.g. to express fondness – *Jonesy* (animals are often given names ending in **y**); to mock, as in *suffragette*.
◆ Ask children to think about nicknames, and abbreviated forms (*William – Bill*).
◆ Brainstorm adjectives that diminish. See the adjectives list below.

Group tasks

◆ Look up origins of affixes in an etymological dictionary and report back. See *Notes*. Make up your own diminutives and define them. What, for instance, might a *lessonette* be? If we have books and Big Books, what about *booklings*? What would you call a tiny crumb? Half a speck of dust? A baby fly?
◆ Play Jigsaw game – create diminutives by fitting together roots and affixes.
◆ Research terms of endearment and baby language (see curiosities list below).

mini	ette	ling	micro	Adjectives	Curiosities
minicomputer	brunette	duckling	microscope	small	Itsy-bitsy
miniature	cigarette	dumpling	microfilm	little	teeny-weenie
miniskirt	majorette	gosling	microchip	tiny	junior
miniscule	kitchenette	sapling	microphone	less	baby
minibus		darling		reduced-	puss-cat
mini-beasts		weakling		low-	diddums
minimum				-kin	pocket-sized
Mini car				-nano	titch

Notes

◆ **ette** is from French, and can have the secondary connotation of being a female version, e.g. *usher, usherette*.
◆ **mini** comes from the Latin *minimus*, meaning 'small'.
◆ **micro** – Latin, meaning 'tiny'.
◆ Be careful with **ling**. It's from old English and can mean 'having a certain quality' as in *weakling*, as well as meaning 'little'.

Year 5 Objectives

**Year 5
Term 1**

Objective 4

To examine the
properties of words
ending in vowels other
than the letter **e**

Whole-class approaches

◆ Using food words from the lists below, brainstorm 'Foods from abroad' and list them in three columns (by endings: **a**, **i**, **o**) with the plural morpheme **s** written in a different colour. Alternatively, distribute food cards and invite children to place their cards under country names written on board. Transfer to world map later. Use the same strategy for 'Unusual animals of the world' or 'Musical words we know'.
◆ Generalise about adding endings.

Group tasks

◆ Make small/concertina booklets entitled: *The A–Z of Italian Food, A Global Glossary of Gorgeous Grub, Around the World in Eighty Animals/Words, An Encyclopaedia of Exciting Eating, Plural Pianos and Singular Sonatas* (musical terms). Use writing frames to encourage use of singular/plural forms.
◆ Write alliterative list poems using plural forms, e.g. Pizzas are perfect for peckish children/Samosas are scrummy for starving school kids.
◆ Use singular/plural flashcards for the Pelmanism game. Differentiate by including regular/irregular forms in the pack.

LIST 1					
anacondas	corgis	haikus	patios	siestas	yoyos
areas	cuckoos	igloos	pianos	skis	zulus
armadillos	dahlias	jumbos	piccolos	sofas	zoos
bananas	dingos	kangaroos	piazzas	sombreros	
banjos	discos	kiwis	pizzas	solos	
bhajis	ecus	kimonos	pumas	sonatas	
bongos	emus	magnolias	radios	tattoos	
cameras	fiestas	matzos	risottos	tarantulas	
casinos	galas	oratorios	rotas	tombolas	
cellos	geckos	paellas	sambas	umbrellas	
chapattis	gnus	pagodas	samosas	violas	
concertos	gurus	pastas	saunas	visas	

LIST 2					
buffaloes	dominoes	heroes	torpedoes	vetoes	volcanoes
cargoes	echoes	haloes	mangoes	flamingoes	

LIST 3				
antennae	bacteria	criteria	fungi	phenomena
macaroni	ravioli	spaghetti	tagliatelli	strata

Notes

◆ Most nouns ending in **o** form their plural by adding **s**, especially musical terms, words recently introduced from other languages, abbreviations, and words ending in two vowels. There are some exceptions to this rule when **es** is added to form the plural (List 2).
◆ A few words keep the plural spelling of the original language (List 3). Some pasta terms are already plurals in Italian!
◆ Some of these words may be unknown to your class, but they have been included to serve a range of languages you may have in your classroom.

Year 5
Term 1

Objective 5 (1 of 2)

To investigate, collect and classify spelling patterns in pluralisation, construct rules for regular spellings, e.g. add **s** to most words; add **es** to most words ending in **s**, **sh**, **ch**; when **y** is preceded by a consonant, change to **ies**; when **y** is preceded by a vowel, add **s**

Whole-class approaches
◆ Create a list of singulars with their plurals, either by brainstorming, collecting over time or using the lists below. Ask children to group them according to the way they add or change their endings to accommodate the plural.
◆ Use 'show me' cards for **s/es** endings. Children show the correct ending in response to an oral word.
◆ Individual whiteboards – children attempt to apply taught rules in response to a given word.
◆ Cloze passage featuring deleted plurals.

Group tasks
◆ Investigation – after establishing the basic 'Add **s**' rule, children could conduct and open investigation into other ways of forming plurals.
◆ Do word sums, e.g. *cargo* + **s** = _____ ; *babies* – **s** = _____
◆ Play a card game or bingo featuring cards with pluralisation rules written in the squares, and in which cards are drawn featuring different words to be pluralised.
◆ Design posters or radio commercials to advertise a spelling rule.

Extension activities
◆ Investigate:
  ◆ words that have no singular (e.g. *trousers, scissors*);
  ◆ words that are the same in the singular and plural (e.g. *sheep, deer*);
  ◆ plurals with endings other than **s** (e.g. *mice, men*);
  ◆ plurals of words ending in **o** (e.g. *potatoes, tomatoes*).

Typical words		Hissing and buzzing words		Consonant + **y** words	
dog	dogs	hiss	hisses	city	cities
house	houses	bus	buses	try	tries
meal	meals	church	churches	lorry	lorries
balloon	balloons	dish	dishes	worry	worries
sister	sisters	lunch	lunches	cry	cries
school	schools	fox	foxes	baby	babies
day	days	box	boxes	party	parties
word	words	watch	watches	puppies	puppies
boy	boys	fish	fishes	lolly	lollies
girl	girls	patch	patches	jelly	jellies

Notes
◆ Most nouns add **s** in the plural.
◆ Nouns ending in hissing, buzzing or shushing sounds (**s/x/ch/sh**) add **es** in the plural. This adds a syllable and makes it easier to say.
◆ Nouns ending in consonant + **y** change **y** to **i** and add **es**. Compare nouns ending in vowel + **y** which simply add **s**.
◆ Several nouns ending in **o** add **es** in the plural. These tend to be older words, e.g. *potatoes*. Newer words like *patio* and *radio* add **s** in the plural.

Year 5
Term 1

Objective 5 (2 of 2)

To investigate, collect and classify spelling patterns in pluralisation, e.g. change **f** to **ves**

Whole-class approaches

◆ Create a list of singulars with their plurals, either by brainstorming, collecting over time or by using the lists below. Invite children to group them according to the way they add and change their endings to accommodate the plural.
◆ Use 'show me' cards for **s/es** endings. Children show the correct ending in response to an oral word.
◆ Individual whiteboards: children attempt to apply taught rules in response to a given word.
◆ Cloze passage featuring deleted plurals.

Group tasks

◆ Investigation – after establishing the basic 'Add **s**' rule, children could conduct an open investigation into other ways of forming plurals.
◆ Word sums, e.g. *self* + **s** = _____
◆ Play card game or bingo featuring cards with pluralisation rules written in the squares, and in which cards are drawn featuring different words to be pluralised.
◆ Design posters or radio commercials to advertise a spelling rule.

Extension activities

◆ words that have no singular (e.g. *trousers, scissors*);
◆ words that are the same in the singular and plural (e.g. *sheep, deer*);
◆ plurals with endings other than **s** (e.g. *mice, men*);
◆ plurals of words ending in **o** (e.g. *potatoes, tomatoes*).

f and fe endings		Irregular plurals	
calf	calves	antenna	antennae
self	selves	goose	geese
thief	thieves	man	men
half	halves	woman	women
wolf	wolves	mouse	mice
knife	knives	louse	lice
loaf	loaves	die	dice
life	lives	tooth	teeth
scarf	scarves	child	children
wife	wives	formula	formulae

Notes

◆ Many nouns ending in **f** drop the **f** and add **ves** in the plural. There are exceptions. **ff** words just add **s**, for example.
◆ A number of nouns have unusual plurals. Some change the medial vowel (*goose/geese*); some have retained the plural form of the original language (**a** singular, **ae** plural is Latin).
◆ Several nouns ending in **o** add **es** in the plural. These tend to be older words, e.g. *potatoes*. Newer words like *patio* and *radio* add **s** in the plural.

Year 5 Term 1

Objective 6

To collect and investigate the meanings and spellings of words using the following prefixes: **auto**, **bi**, **trans**, **tele**, **circum**

Whole-class approaches

◆ Write up the prefixes, divide the class into five groups, and ask them to write down as many words as they can in two minutes, for their prefix. Ask them to work out the meaning of the prefix, and teach if unknown.
◆ Play Speedy Dictionaries – pairs race against a 30-second deadline to locate word and origin of a prefix in the dictionary.

Group tasks

◆ Play Kim's game – collecting words with like prefixes.
◆ Play sorting games – for language of origin, for same prefix, scientific words, words linked to movement, etc.
◆ Search dictionary for new phrases like 'automatic focus, automatic door'.
◆ Search Science, Maths and Geography textbooks for examples of words in context.
◆ Do *Yellow Pages* wordsearch for companies which use prefixed words as company name, e.g. AutoGlaze. Try travel and transport companies, etc.
◆ Make links with other languages: words for motorways = *autoroute* (French); *Autobahn* (German); *autopista* (Spanish); *autoput* (Serbo-Croat).

auto	circum	bi	tele	trans
autograph	circumference	biceps	telephone	transmit
autopsy	circumnavigate	bisect	telegraph	transfer
automaton	circumstance	bicycle	telescope	transport
autobiography	circumvent	bifocals	television	transparent
automobile	circulate	bilingual	telepathy	translate
automatic	circus	biplane	telephoto	transatlantic
	circle		Tele Tubbies	transplant
	circular			

Notes

◆ **auto** means 'self'; **circum** means 'round', 'about'; **bi** means 'two' or 'twice'; **tele** means 'distant'; **trans** means 'across'.
◆ Use multicultural opportunities, drawing on other languages in the classroom.

Year 5 Term 1

Objective 8

To identify word roots, derivations, and spelling patterns, e.g. *sign, signature, signal; bomb, bombastic, bombard; remit, permit, permission,* in order to extend vocabulary and provide support for spelling

Whole-class approaches

◆ Using the chart below, provide some examples of word roots and derivations on the board or flipchart. Provide further examples of word roots and ask children to think of words that are derivations. Record these next to the root words. Talk about the fact that many words in the English language are derived from other words and this can provide a clue to their spellings.

◆ Explain that many word roots and derivations are drawn from Latin and Greek, and provide examples of these. In group work, children can investigate the reasons why these two languages have had such an influence on the English language.

Group tasks

◆ Provide each group with cards of root and associated words. Ask the children to sort the words into their relevant families or groups.

◆ Working in pairs, children decide/use a dictionary to check which words in the group are nouns, verbs, adjectives, or adverbs.

◆ Children can develop their own card games, e.g. Beat Your Neighbour for groups of four. Twenty word roots and forty derivations (two per word root) are put onto cards. Each child starts with five word roots. The forty cards of derivations are placed face-down in the middle of the table and children take it in turns to select a word. Unwanted words are placed at the bottom of the pile. The first child to collect five sets of word roots and their derivations and be able to spell all the words in the sets (from memory) wins the game.

act	actor	action	activity	react	reaction
child	children	childhood	childlike	childish	childless
electric	electrical	electricity	electrician	electronic	electrocute
take	mistake	mistaken	overtaken	overtaking	partaking

assist	assistant	assistance	balance	imbalance	unbalanced
bore	boring	boredom	call	recall	calling
claim	reclaim	reclaimable	cover	discover	discovery
examine	examination	examiner	give	given	forgiveness
govern	governor	government	hand	handler	handicraft
hero	heroic	heroism	joy	joyful	enjoyment
light	lightning	delighted	machine	machinery	machinist
medic	medical	medication	obey	disobey	disobedient
operate	cooperate	cooperation	pack	packet	package
pain	painkiller	painstaking	pass	passage	passenger
prison	imprisoned	imprisonment	press	impress	depression
prove	approval	disapprove	public	publication	publicity
relate	relative	relation	shake	shakily	shaken

Note

◆ Encourage use of etymological dictionaries and thesauruses to support children in finding/spelling derivations of words and their origins.

Year 5
Term 2

Objective 4 (1 of 3)

To explore spelling
patterns of consonants
and formulate rules:

- **ll** in *full* becomes **l**
  when used as a suffix

Whole-class approach

◆ Word search in text, or brainstorm. Work out the rule.

Group task

◆ Do a wordsearch.

Extension activity

◆ Investigate if there is a similar effect when **all** and **till** are affixed to other
words.

Typical words					
hope	hopeful	fear	fearful	wake	wakeful
thank	thankful	harm	harmful	scorn	scornful
play	playful	shame	shameful	doubt	doubtful
boast	boastful	faith	faithful	colour	colourful
care	careful	hand	handful	mouth	mouthful

y words					
beauty	beautiful	plenty	plentiful	fancy	fanciful
pity	pitiful	mercy	merciful	bounty	bountiful

Notes

◆ Drop the **l** when adding **full**.
◆ Change **y** to **i** when adding **full**.
◆ Distinguish between 'a hand full of' and 'a handful of'. The first refers to
the hand, the second refers to the quantity.
◆ **all** and **till** also drop the second **l** when they are affixed to other words,
e.g. *always, until*.

Year 5 Term 2

Objective 4 (2 of 3)

To explore spelling patterns of consonants and formulate rules:

- words ending with a single consonant preceded by a short vowel double the consonant before adding **ing**

Whole-class approaches

- ◆ Investigation – use the first group of words to draw a contrast between words that double and those that do not. The clue is in the sound of the preceding vowel.
- ◆ Provide base words and ask children in pairs to spell and show the extended word on a whiteboard.

Group tasks

- ◆ Provide a mixture of base words that were not used in the whole-class activities. Have the children work in pairs to provide the correct spellings when adding **ing**, **er**, **ed**, **est** where appropriate.
- ◆ Provide children with newspaper or magazine articles. Ask them to find, highlight and record words that have consonants doubled where suffixes have been added.

Contrasting sets

hop	hopping	hopped	hope	hoping	hoped
dine	diner	dinner	write	writer	written
hid	hide	hidden	ride	rider	ridden
care	caring	careful	carry	carrying	carried

Doubled letters

beg	begged	beggar	big	bigger	biggest
dig	digging	digger	drag	dragging	dragged
drop	dropping	dropped	mop	mopping	mopped
hum	humming	hummed	hug	hugging	hugged
run	runner	running	stop	stopper	stopped
sun	sunny	sunnier	fit	fitter	fittest
win	winning	winner	wet	wetter	wettest

Undoubled letters

beep	beeping	beeped	blast	blasting	blasted
burn	burner	burning	count	counter	counted
disgust	disgusted	disgusting	dream	dreamer	dreaming
feel	feeling	feeler	help	helped	helper
train	trainer	trained	trick	tricky	tricked

Notes

- ◆ Ensure that children understand the difference between short- and long-vowel sounds.
- ◆ When you are providing examples of words with short- and long-vowel sounds, emphasise or exaggerate the sounding out and have the children join in.
- ◆ Short (rap) vowel = double consonant.
- ◆ Long vowel = single consonant.

Year 5 Term 2

Objective 4 (3 of 3)

To explore spelling patterns of consonants and formulate rules:
- **c** is usually soft when followed by **i**, e.g. *circus, accident*

Whole-class approaches

◆ By investigation – use lists of words for **ca**, **ce**, **ci**, **co** and **cu**, and ask children to generalise about the way the words sound. Ask them to read aloud – to hear the difference and find the pattern.

◆ Alternatively, ask the children to brainstorm and decide what rules apply for words with the **ca**, **ce**, **ci**, **co** and **cu** pattern, e.g.

call, calendar, camera, cardigan, carnival, recap
celery, centimetre, centre, cereal, centipede, descend
circle, cinema, cinnamon, decide
coat, cobweb, coffin, cold, column, cow, disco
cupboard, curtain, custard, customer, cut, discuss

Have them decide which other **c** group belongs with the **ci** group, i.e. **ce**.

Group tasks

◆ Independent investigation – give the children a group of cards containing a mix of **c** words and ask them to sort the words and work out the rule for themselves about the vowel following **c**.

◆ Have the children find as many words as they can from the different **c** + vowel groups.

Extension activity

◆ Ask the children to find and record examples of **cy** words (which also have the soft **c** sound).

ci					
cinema	cinnamon	circle	circuit	circular	circulation
circumference	circumstance	circus	incisor	cistern	citizen
city	accident	civil	decide	decision	decisive
decimal	incident	disciple	discipline	recite	recital

ce					
ceiling	celebrate	celebrity	celery	cell	cellar
cellophane	certain	cement	cemetery	census	cent
centenary	centigrade	centipede	recent	centre	century
cereal	ceremony	incense	certificate	deceased	deceit
December	decent	descend	discern	except	receive

cy					
cyanide	bicycle	cyclist	cyclone	cylinder	fancy
cynic	cynical	cypress	cyst	mercy	lacy

Notes

◆ **ci**, **ce** and **cy** usually soften the **c**.
◆ Exception for **ce** – Celt, Celtic – pronounced as Kelt, Keltic.

Year 5
Term 2

Objective 5

To investigate words that have common letter strings but different pronunciations, e.g. *rough, cough, bough; boot, foot*

Whole-class approaches
◆ Write word groups on the board and ask the children to sort them by sound.
◆ Postboxes – post words into the correct box.
◆ Investigation – what effect do preceding and following letters have on the pronunciation of the string?

Group tasks
◆ Do word sorts.
◆ Play card games, collecting up similar sounds.
◆ Word ladders – children build a word around the string by changing or adding only <u>one</u> letter each turn, e.g. *cough – rough – bough – bought – brought.*

ight	ear	oo	ough	ie	our
right	pear	book	bough	lie	armour
fight	bear	boot	cough	pie	colour
light	rear	cook	dough	tie	favour
night	beard	food	enough	fried	honour
eight	search	foot	plough	lied	neighbour
weight	fear	good	though	tried	rumour
height	wear	hood	bought	niece	pour
freight	year	hook	brought	piece	your
tight	tear	hoot	drought	field	hour
	dear	look	sought	shield	flour
	near	loot	thought	grieve	
	learn	mood	wrought	thieves	
	earn	nook			
	yearn	pool			
	gear	rook			
	ear	root			
	hear	soot			
	heard	took			
	clear				
	hearth				
	earth				
	heart				

Notes
◆ This objective extends the earlier teaching that, just as a phoneme can be spelled in more than one way, the same spelling may represent more than one phoneme.
◆ Use the lists to demonstrate how:
  ◆ pronunciation often depends on preceding and following sounds, e.g. an **e** before **igh** usually gives it a long 'ay' sound;
  ◆ (**ie** list) **i** interacts with other letters as part of a phoneme (e.g. *thief*) when its sound is unpredictable, and as a modified **y** (e.g. *fried*) when its sound is always **i**;
  ◆ Usage can also depend on dialect (the **our** list is useful here).

Year 5
Term 2

Objective 6

To distinguish between homophones, i.e. words with common pronunciations but different spellings, e.g. *eight, ate; grate, great; rain, rein, reign*

Whole-class approaches
◆ Teach words and meaning directly, and display.
◆ Place Post-It notes over homophones in shared texts and ask children to work out which one fits.
◆ Make individual flashcards (e.g. *there/their*) for children and ask them to hold up the correct spelling in response to a sentence in which the meaning is clear.
◆ Riddles – 'What opens locks and is always found beside water?'

Group tasks
◆ Play Kim's game – place cards face-down and hunt out the pairs. You can claim a pair if you can prove you know the correct meaning using a dictionary.
◆ Play Sound Snap with a limited number of priority words.
◆ Invent mnemonics and ways of working out the correct choice.
◆ Play Beat the Spellchecker – write a 100-word story or report that beats the spellchecker. Team with the most cheats wins.

Extension activities
◆ Look for homonyms (same spelling, different meanings, e.g. *bear*).
◆ Research history of words to explain the origin of some homophones spellings.

rein	rain	reign	you	yew	ewe
rode	road	rowed	too	two	to
by	buy	bye	their	they're	there
sew	so	sow	cent	scent	sent

cell	sell	made	maid	cereal	serial
dear	deer	main	mane	key	quay
beach	beech	meet	meat	scene	seen
blue	blew	pane	pain	vain	vein
grate	great	peace	piece	waist	waste
hair	hare	plane	plain	fate	fete
here	hear	sum	some	flour	flower
herd	heard	read	red	bean	been
him	hymn	right	write	week	weak
hour	our	break	brake	leak	leek
knight	night	steel	steal	aloud	allowed
knot	not	stair	stare	board	bored
know	no	tail	tale	sun	son

Notes
◆ Many homophone choices are best taught as a grammatical issue, e.g. *there/their*.
◆ Note that analogy with family groups can be helpful, e.g. *ear, hear, heard; here, where, there*.

Year 5 Term 2

Objective 7

The correct use and spelling of possessive pronouns, linked to work on grammar, e.g. *their, theirs; your, yours; my, mine*

Whole-class approaches

◆ Write on the board an incomplete list of possessive pronouns. Ask children to complete the pattern, then discuss what the pronouns have in common, e.g. they tell us who things belong to; they don't use people's names; they represent people's names. Identify the function of the words. Explain the name 'pronoun'.
◆ In Shared Reading and Writing, invite children to substitute pronouns for nouns, using pronoun 'show me' fans.
◆ Search for words within words, e.g. y**our**s, m**in**e.

Group tasks

◆ Investigate the pattern by which the words in column 2 are followed by nouns, while those in column 3 stand alone.
◆ Make Who Am I?, Who Are They? and Who Are We? guessing-game cards, using the possessive pronouns, e.g. 'Our noses are long, our skin is grey, our memories are long. Who are we? Elephants.'
◆ Pronoun hunt – where in sentences do pronouns tend to arise? How do they work in relation to the named person?
◆ Create lines or poems based on possessive pronouns, e.g. 'your loss, my lucky find'.

Extension activities

◆ Research older forms of pronouns, e.g. *thee/thine*.
◆ Research pronouns in other languages, e.g. *ta/ton; mein/meine*.

I	my	mine
you	your	yours
he	his	his
she	her	hers
it	its	its
we	our	ours
they	their	theirs

Note

◆ *It's* = it is; *its* = belonging to it.

Year 5 Term 2

Objective 8

To recognise and spell the suffix: **cian**, etc.

Whole-class approaches

◆ Make class collections of 'shun' words. Categorise them according to word ending (see lists below).
◆ Develop and draw out patterns leading to general rules determining spelling pattern (see *Notes* below).
◆ Give a base word and ask children to write the correct 'shun' suffix, e.g. *educate, magic*. Alternatively, use a 'shun' fan for children to flash in response.

Group tasks

◆ Suffix wheels – one child turns the wheel to move a suffix, into a window on the card, partner has to think of a 'shun' word with that suffix (checked in dictionary).
◆ Word building – roots and suffixes for 'shun' words on separate cards – children have to match roots and suffixes to complete words correctly.
◆ Sorting activities – sort cards into piles, e.g. **tion** words into five piles depending on the preceding vowel, e.g. **ation**, **etion**, etc. Generalise and explain. (See *Notes*.)

cian	sion	ssion	tion	other
physician	extension	profession	fiction	Venetian
optician	collision	session	fraction	Ocean
magician	confusion	percussion	direction	Asian
politician	exclusion	discussion	attention	Russian
electrician	transfusion	oppression	proportion	
	infusion	passion	reduction	
	explosion	mission	mansion	
	corrosion	possession	diction	

ation	etion	ition	otion	ution
nation	completion	repetition	motion	distribution
station	deletion	competition	lotion	pollution
foundation		opposition	devotion	revolution
education		position	promotion	institution
translation		petition	emotion	constitution
demonstration		intuition		contribution

Notes

◆ **cian** – where words end in **c**; common in occupations.
◆ **tion** – the most common ending.
◆ **sion** – where the base word ends in **d/de** or **s/se** (e.g. *explode, confuse*).
◆ **ssion** – clear soft 'sh' sound.
◆ **ation** – long **a** is always followed by **tion**.
◆ **otion/ution/etion** – the base word usually contains the vowel, clearly pronounced.
◆ **ution** words are usually longer than three syllables; **usion** tends to be shorter.

Year 5
Term 3

Objective 4

To spell unstressed vowels in polysyllabic words, e.g. *company, portable, poisonous, interest, description, carpet, sector, freedom, extra*, etc.

Whole-class approaches

◆ Select a group of words that contain unstressed vowels and write them on the board or flip chart. Ask the children to work out what the words have in common and why people might have difficulty in spelling these words.

◆ Ask for suggestions as to how the spellings of such words could be memorised, e.g. exaggerated pronunciation where words are broken down into syllables – *diff-er-ence*; thinking of the root word, e.g. *differ* + the suffix *ence* use of mnemonics, e.g. '*pet* on the car*pet*', '*Al* is in hospit*al*'.

Group tasks

◆ Children work in pairs to develop further ideas/mnemonics for supporting the spelling of words provided in the chart below.

◆ Ask the children to decide on categories for grouping the words, e.g. **ary**, **ery**, **ory**, **erence**.

◆ Children select a number of words from the categories which have prefixes and find the root word. They then repeat this activity with words that have suffixes and finally with words that have both prefixes and suffixes.

abandoned	abominable	original	predict	familiar	carpet
animal	description	boundary	business	stationary	stationery
category	catholic	poisonous	centre	company	compromise
conference	offering	deafening	desperate	definite	definitely
dictionary	difference	different	doctor	prosperous	easily
explanatory	extra	factory	family	secretary	primary
flattery	smuggler	formal	freedom	frightening	general
generally	generous	Wednesday	heaven	hospital	separate
widening	interest	disinterest	interested	jewellery	voluntary
library	literacy	literate	illiterate	literature	lottery
marvellous	miserable	memorable	reference	messenger	prepare

Notes

◆ Draw children's attention to the high number of words that contain the **er** and **en** patterns.

◆ Children can be supported in remembering the different spellings for *stationary* and *stationery* by using the mnemonic 'buy stationery from the stationer'.

◆ Helpful tactics:
  ◆ refer to root;
  ◆ build the word up to detect prefixes and suffixes, and syllables;
  ◆ refer to related words, e.g. *definite – finite;*
  ◆ say words as they might sound, e.g. *Wed–nes–day*.

Year 5
Term 3

Objective 5 (1 of 3)

To investigate and learn spelling rules:
- words ending in modifying **e** drop **e** when adding **ing**, e.g. *taking*
- words ending in modifying **e** keep **e** when adding a suffix beginning with a consonant, e.g. *hopeful, lovely*

Whole-class approaches
◆ Generate a list of base words ending in a modifying **e** (i.e. the **e** is part of a vowel digraph which make a long-vowel sound on the preceding vowel), and their suffixes. Compare the effect of adding suffixes that begin with a vowel and others that begin with a consonant.

Group task
◆ Mix and match a handful of base words with different suffixes. See below.

Useful exemplars				
live	living	lived	lively	lifeless
hope	hoping	hoped	hopeful	hopeless
care	caring	cared	careful	careless
shame	shaming	shamed	shameful	shameless
tune	tuning	tuned	tuneful	tuneless

Useful base words		Vowel suffixes		Consonant suffixes
sure	love	ing	est	ful
rehearse	age	ed	ism	ment
nice	use	ish	able	less
save	pave	er	al	ness
				ly

Notes
◆ Drop the **e** to add vowel suffixes.
◆ Retain the **e** to add consonant suffixes.

Year 5 Term 3

Objective 5 (2 of 3)

To investigate and learn spelling rules:

- words ending in **y** preceded by a consonant change **y** to **ie** when adding a suffix, e.g. *flies, tried* – except for the suffixes **ly** or **ing**, e.g. *shyly, flying*

Whole-class approaches

- ◆ Investigation – sort words and work out the rule.
- ◆ Fill out the lines of a grid (like the first batch of words in the one below), halting at the modified letters, to generalise.
- ◆ Demonstrate the adding of suffixes, then give children a key word (e.g. *funny*) to work on their whiteboards.

Group tasks

- ◆ Children work in pairs to fill in or complete a prepared grid.
- ◆ Investigation – sorting words and generalising.
- ◆ Finding the obvious and less obvious suffixes which go on verbs (see second batch below).

Extension activities

- ◆ investigate words ending in vowel + **y**;
- ◆ investigate whether the final letter changes in any other word when adding a suffix (alphabetically, e.g. *stamina, scab, panic, card, concrete, stiff, flag, fish,* etc.)

Adjectives				
happy	happiness	happier	happiest	happily
pretty	prettiness	prettier	prettiest	prettily
lazy	laziness	lazier	laziest	lazily
hungry	hungriness	hungrier	hungriest	hungrily
windy	windiness	windier	windiest	windily
ready	readiness	readier	readiest	readily
heavy	heaviness	heavier	heaviest	heavily
empty	emptiness	emptier	emptiest	emptily

Verbs					
supply	supplying	supplied	supplicant	supplier	
carry	carrying	carried	carrier	carriage	
marry	marrying	married	marriage		
try	trying	tried	trial		
ally	allying	allied	alliance		
vary	varying	varied	variety	variation	variable
reply	replying	replied	replicate	replication	replica

Notes

- ◆ **y** changes to **i** when you add the suffixes **ness**, **er**, **est**, **ed**, **ly**.
- ◆ An important exception is adding **ing** – it would be very odd to have a word containing a double **i**, and difficult to say.
- ◆ No other final letter changes when adding a suffix (though letters can double).

Year 5
Term 3

Objective 5 (3 of 3)

To investigate and learn spelling rules:
• **i** before **e** except after **c** when the sound is 'ee', e.g. *receive*. Note and learn exceptions

Whole-class approaches
◆ Generate a list of words in which **i** and **e** are adjacent and invite children to search for patterns. Remind children that both digraphs can make different sounds, some of which overlap.
◆ Use 'show me' cards featuring **ei** and **ie** which children can show in response to a given oral word.

Group tasks
◆ Investigation – collect words and find patterns to prime the whole-class session.
◆ Create a poster to advertise guidelines for choosing the correct digraph.
◆ Investigation – find as many ways of sounding **ie** as possible, with examples. Likewise with **a**. Which are common and which are unique to each digraph?

ie			cei	ei (long a)	ei (other)
lie	chief	shield	ceiling	vein	weird
die	handkerchief	shriek	receive	rein	protein
pie	pierce	yield	receipt	reign	their
tie	field	niece	deceit	veil	either
thief	priest	relief	perceive	weigh	neither
belief	fierce	pier	conceit	freight	height
grief	mischief	patient		eight	heir
brief	quiet	view		neighbour	
piece	friend	ancient		sovereign	
review	medieval	glacier		foreign	
fiery	obedient	science			

Notes
◆ Most words use **ie**.
◆ **ie** is the only word-ending.
◆ **ei** is the only word-beginning.
◆ **c** is usually followed by **ei** (*science, glacier* and *ancient* are troublesome exceptions).
◆ The long **a** sound generally indicates **ei**. Note that the long **a** pronunciation has drifted a little over time, and is also influenced by accent.
◆ Other common **ei** words (see chart, final column) are best memorised by exception.

Year 5
Term 3

Objective 6

To transform words, e.g. changing tenses: **ed**, **ing**; negation: **un**, **im**, **il**; making comparatives: **er**, **est**, **ish**; changing verbs to nouns, e.g. **ion**, **ism**, **ology**; nouns to verbs: **ise**, **ify**, **en**

Whole-class approaches

◆ Use a number of base words to generate examples of how a word may change its meaning and spelling when it is transformed by adding suffixes and prefixes. Ask children to identify 'when' and 'why' words:
  ◆ use particular endings, e.g. **ise** to create a verb, **il** to negate a word beginning with **l**;
  ◆ tend to modify their spelling, e.g. words ending in **e** and **y**.

Group tasks

◆ Race to collect the base words with most different forms.
◆ Each group specialises in one aspect, e.g. words ending in **y**; words changing into nouns to report back to the plenary.

Extension activity

◆ Investigate how the same job might be done by adding a word, e.g. **er** by more, **est** by most).

Base words			Negation	Verb to noun	Noun to verb
love	arm	help	un	tion	ise
hate	care	small	de	ism	ify
change	critic	art	dis	ness	ate
class	age	magnet	anti	ity	en
press	fool	possible	il	ist	
child	medicine	legal		ir	
educate	responsible	happy		im	
long	kind	mobile		in	
possible	decide	television			
reduce	compose	simple			

Tense	Comparatives
s/es	er
d/ed	est
ing	ish
en	like

Note

◆ See activities for some earlier objectives in this booklet (Y3/T1/O10 – page 6, Y3/T2/O8 – page 8, Y4/T1/O7 – page 23, Y4/T1/O14 – page 27, Y4/T3/O8 – page 36).

Year 5 Term 3

Objective 7

To recognise the spelling and meaning of the prefixes: **in**, **im**, **ir**, **il**, **pro**, **sus**

Whole-class approaches

◆ Teach words and meanings directly, and display.
◆ Present lists and investigate spelling patterns.
◆ Write lists of words, then cover up the prefixes – choose which prefix will work.

Group task

◆ Collect more words using alphabetical list in the *Penguin Rhyming Dictionary*.

Extension activities

◆ Produce a set of insults for use in a drama activity in which children bandy insults in a row, choosing words from the **in**, **ir** and **im** lists, then compare them with insults which characters in Romeo and Juliet hurl at each other!
◆ Investigate the use of **un**, **dis**, **de** and **anti**.

in	im	ir	il	pro	sus
inactive	immature	irregular	illegal	proactive	suspect
indecent	immobile	irrational	illiterate	project	suspense
incapable	impractical	irresponsible	illegible	provide	suspicion
inconvenient	impossible	irresistible		produce	suspend
inattentive	improbable			propose	sustain
incredible	improper			proceed	
inverted	impatient			propeller	
inaccurate	impolite				

Notes

◆ **in** means 'not'.
◆ **ir** means 'not' – add to the beginning of words beginning with **r**, thus producing double **r**. Note several exceptions, however, e.g. *unreasonable*.
◆ **il** means 'not' – add to beginning of words beginning with **l**, thus producing double **l**. Note several exceptions, however, e.g. *dislike, unload*.
◆ **im** means 'not' – add to the beginning of words beginning with **m** and **p**. Note several exceptions, however, e.g. *unmade, displease*.
◆ **sus** – a version of **sub** meaning 'under', but the meaning has drifted from being 'under the spotlight' in *suspect* to being 'held up' in *suspend*.
◆ **pro** means 'ahead'.
◆ Note the double letters created when the prefix is added to words beginning with the same letter.
◆ Words containing the letter string conform to the rules even though they lack the root meaning, e.g. *illuminate, illustrate, irritate, irrigate*.

Year 6 Objectives

Year 6 Term 1

Objective 5

To use word roots, prefixes and suffixes as a support for spelling, e.g. **aero**, **aqua**, **audi**, **bi**, **cede**, **clude**, **con**, **cred**, **duo**, **log(o)(y)**, **hyd(ro)(ra)**, **in**, **micro**, **oct**, **photo**, **port**, **prim**, **scribe**, **scope**, **sub**, **tele**, **tri**, **ex**

Whole-class approaches

◆ Investigation – provide a number of words using the same root and invite children to identify the common root and its meaning.

◆ Give the root and its meaning and ask children to generate a list of words which contain both the letters and the meaning.

◆ Provide cards containing common prefixes, roots and suffixes, and ask children to construct known words from these.

Group tasks

◆ Use dictionaries to research and establish clusters of words using the same root.

◆ Create new words, e.g. *aquaphone*.

◆ Use etymological dictionary to research word histories.

◆ Investigate words based on numbers and research background, e.g. **octo** means 'eight' (Latin).

◆ Investigate other roots – e.g. **cede** ('yield'), **clude** ('shut'), **con** ('together'), **cred** ('belief'), **duo** ('two'), **hydro/a** ('water'), **photo** ('light'), **port** ('carry'), **scrib/p** ('write'), **scope** ('look'), **sub** ('under'), **tri** ('three'), **ex** ('outside').

bi	*two*	bicycle	biped	binoculars	binary
aqua	*water*	aquarium	Aquarius	aquatic	aquaplane
aero	*air*	aeroplane	aerodrome	aeronauts	aerodynamic
super	*greater*	supernatural	Superman	supernova	superpower
micro	*small*	microscope	microfilm	microphone	microcosm
audi	*hear*	audible	audience	audition	auditorium
port	*carry*	transport	portable	import	export
trans	*across*	transport	transplant	transfer	transaction
prim	*first*	prime	primary	primrose	primate
auto	*self*	automatic	autograph	autobiography	automobile
phobia	*fear*	claustrophobia	arachnophobia	agoraphobia	xenophobia
ology	*study*	archaeology	biology	geology	zoology
tele	*far off*	telephone	television	teleport	telecom
graph	*to write*	autograph	telegraph	photograph	graphic
re	*again*	replay	reply	reconsider	repeat
pre	*before*	preview	prehistoric	previous	prevent

Year 6 Term 1

Objective 6

To investigate meanings and spellings of connectives: *therefore, notwithstanding, furthermore,* etc.; link to Sentence Level work on connectives

Whole-class approaches

◆ Start from a known text such as a report or journalistic writing. Highlight connectives and help class to work out their function – to connect.
◆ Identify phrases used as connectives, e.g. 'in addition', 'on the other hand'.
◆ Try substituting different connectives and consider how they change the meaning.
◆ Look at the position of the connective words or phrases. Where do they come in the sentence?
◆ Consider their features as words:
    ◆ some are simple words like *and, so, but*;
    ◆ some are connective phrases like *in addition to*;
    ◆ some are compound words (possibly derived from phrases) like *notwithstanding*.

Group tasks

◆ Ask children to categorise connectives into simple and compound words. Compound words could be further split into two- and three-part words.
◆ Looking at the compound-word connectives, work out unknown meanings by looking at the separate parts of the word. Use a dictionary to check.

Extension activity

◆ Use a King James Bible or other old text such as a legal document, to find further connectives, e.g. *hereafter, howsoever, whomsoever*.

furthermore	then	however	so	nonetheless
but	because	therefore	and	moreover
henceforward	whenever	as	with	meanwhile
notwithstanding	after	when	although	if
since	nevertheless	while	besides	whatever
until	yet	for	consequently	whoever
whereas	alternatively			

Notes

◆ Connectives are words (or phrases) that can be used to link one sentence to another or to extend sentences.
◆ A connective can be a conjunction, an adverb or an adverbial phrase.
◆ Compound connectives behave like other compound words; that is, the two (or three) original words don't change their spelling.

Appendix 1
Spelling around the clock

PLENARY
- Presentation of investigation results.

SHARED READING
- Finding patterns and examples.
- Reminders of spelling patterns previously taught.
- Incidental words of interest.

SHARED WRITING
- Constructing words from phonemes.
- Modelling strategies to construct unknown words.

GUIDED WRITING
- Applying strategies to unknown words.
- Personal guidance about specific spelling problems.

INDEPENDENT WORK
- Group investigations.
- Using self-help strategies, dictionaries, etc.
- Spelling games and activities.
- Peer support to learn, revise and test spellings.

WORD LEVEL
- Learning spelling rules.
- Investigating spelling patterns.
- Learning spelling strategies.

Appendix 2
Teaching spelling conventions

Tell the children the objective.

Introduce a set of relevant words.

Ask children to sort the words and identify patterns.

Help children to hypothesise and test their ideas.

Explain the principle behind the pattern, if appropriate.

Practise the convention.

Explore and extend, e.g. exceptions, variations, applications.

Using investigations

Benefits of working through investigation:
- ◆ It appeals to problem-solving instincts.
- ◆ It obliges children to be more active in deconstructing words.
- ◆ It models a useful self-help strategy.
- ◆ It makes conventions more rational.

Limitations of working through investigation:
- ◆ It depends on having a useful list of words.
- ◆ Children may not see a pattern or be able to explain it.
- ◆ Some rules are too complex for this treatment.
- ◆ You have to understand the rule yourself.
- ◆ Exceptions must be dealt with.

As an independent group activity:
- ◆ The word source must be reliable.
- ◆ The children may need helpful prompts or guides in case they get stuck.
- ◆ It needs to be checked, e.g. in a plenary.

Appendix 3
Examples of investigations

SHARED INVESTIGATION (teacher led)
Investigate the adding of **ing** to words

Year 3
Term 1

Objective 8

How the spellings of verbs alter when **ing** is added

Prompts
1 Look at my list of words (see column 1). How would I change *clean* to *cleaning*? *See* to *seeing*? etc. Amend to become column 2.
2 If in doubt, just add **ing**. Most words do.
3 Here are some words (see columns 3 and 4) which do something rather odd when we add **ing**. What happens? Can you work out why this happens? What do they have in common? Further prompt: Look at the sound before the double letter.
4 Words which have a short (rap) vowel before the final consonant double it. It's useful for the reader too – s/he can see that the vowel is short.
5 Here's another group of words (see columns 5 and 6 – split digraphs) which do something different. What happens?
6 Does our other rule still hold good in this list? (Short vowels create doubles, long vowels don't). The rule does hold good.
7 Tell me three rules about adding **ing**, completing these sentences:
   – Most words …
   – A short (rap) vowel just before the end tells us …
   – Words ending in **e** will …

Simple – add **ing**		Short vowels – double		Drop **e** + add **ing**	
clean	cleaning	hop	hopping	hope	hoping
think	thinking	shop	shopping	take	taking
dream	dreaming	shut	shutting	write	writing
say	saying	hug	hugging	bite	biting
do	doing	plan	planning	share	sharing
walk	walking	clap	clapping	decide	deciding
go	going	chat	chatting	drive	driving
send	sending	let	letting	care	caring
pack	packing	fit	fitting	make	making
jump	jumping	skip	skipping	save	saving
ask	asking	run	running	shine	shining

Notes
◆ Most words just add **ing**.
◆ Words ending in **e** drop the **e** to add **ing**. (Caution: The dropped **e** applies to split digraphs – 'Magic **e**'. It doesn't apply to other **e** endings – *seeing, being, freeing* – but as these are all high-frequency words, children don't usually suffer confusion about this. It is probably best to leave it unless children raise it or start making the error.)
◆ Words with a short vowel before the final letter double the final letter.

Year 3
Term 2

Objective 9

To investigate and identify basic rules for changing the spelling of nouns when **s** is added

INDEPENDENT INVESTIGATION (working without the teacher)
Adding **s** to make a plural

Prompts

1 Cut up the words so they are still in pairs, i.e. *ash* and *ashes* on one card.
2 Your first job is to work out how you decide whether to add **s** or **es** to the end of a word.
3 Make two lists with your words – those ending in **s** and those ending in **es**.
4 Look carefully at the **es** list and make new groups for different endings, e.g. words ending in **x**.
5 Read the **es** lists aloud. What can you hear?
6 Try saying the **es** words without the **e**. Why is this difficult?
7 Write a rule about which endings need an **es**.
8 Check it by trying it on other words you know.
9 Try clapping out the syllables in your **es** lists. What happens when you add **es**? Does the same thing happen to words in the **s** column?
10 Look closely at the list of words ending in **s**. What rules can you work out for adding **s** to:
   – words ending in **e**;
   – words ending in **y** (two rules here);
   – words ending in other letters.
11 Make a list of your own words ending in **f**. Can you work out what happens to these when you add **s**?

ash	ashes	box	boxes	brush	brushes
bush	bushes	church	churches	dish	dishes
glass	glasses	inch	inches	kiss	kisses
watch	watches	sandwich	sandwiches	tax	taxes
game	games	fox	foxes	witch	witches
table	tables	rope	ropes	shoe	shoes
pen	pens	time	times	tune	tunes
cup	cups	bean	beans	tick	ticks
pond	ponds	pocket	pockets	school	schools
book	books	window	windows	lip	lips
desk	desks	clasp	clasps	hat	hats
army	armies	party	parties	baby	babies
berry	berries	city	cities	fly	flies
jelly	jellies	penny	pennies	puppy	puppies
boy	boys	toy	toys	key	keys
ray	rays	display	displays	monkey	monkeys
delay	delays	day	days	donkey	donkeys

Notes

◆ Most words add **s**.
◆ Add **es** if the word ends in a hissing/buzzing/shushing sound. Another way to remember this is to add **es** if you can hear an extra syllable when you make it plural. (The **e** is added to make the plural easier on the tongue, putting a buffer between too many **s** sounds.)
◆ Words ending in **e** – just add **s**.
◆ Words ending in **y** – add **s** if the final letter is preceded by a vowel. If not, change the **y** to **i** and add **es**.

Year 4
Term 1

Objective 5

To spell two-syllable words containing consonants, e.g. *bubble, kettle, common*

SHARED INVESTIGATION (teacher led)
To spell two-syllable words containing double consonants

Prompts

1 Read aloud these pairs of words.
2 How many syllables in each word? (Try clapping.)
3 Come out and underline the first vowel in each word.
4 Read aloud this first pair and tell me what happens to the sound of that vowel.
5 Let's listen to the rest of the words. What happens?
6 Can anyone see a link between the sound of the vowel and the spelling of the word?
7 What kind of vowel comes before a double letter?
8 What happens if it's a long vowel?
9 Tell me the rule as simply as you can.
10 Can you think of any more examples of double letters in a two-syllable word?

For comparing sounds		Further examples		
diner	dinner	common	rotten	letter
biter	bitter	follow	sudden	stopped
coma	comma	daddy	puppy	summer
writing	written	pillow	swallow	carry
taping	tapping	funny	running	happy
pole	pollen	tennis	better	gobble
hoping	hopping	swimming	penny	mummy
super	supper	shopping	getting	silly
lady	laddy	winner	butter	cotton
slope	sloppy	sorry	kitten	kettle

Notes

◆ The children need to understand the short (rap) vowel sounds:
   a as in ant;
   e as in egg;
   i as in ink;
   o as in orange;
   u as in umbrella.
◆ Long vowels say their own name.
◆ Short (rap) vowels are followed by double consonants; long vowels are followed by single consonants.

Year 4
Term 2

Objective 5

To investigate what happens to words ending in **f** when suffixes are added

INDEPENDENT INVESTIGATION (working without the teacher)
Extending words which end in **f**

Prompts
1 Brainstorm three lists of words which end in **ff**, **f** or **fe**.
2 Split each list into nouns and verbs.
3 Put the nouns into the plural. Check the spellings in a spelling dictionary. Work out the rule about putting each list into the plural.
4 Put the verbs into different tenses by adding **s**, **ing** and **ed**. Work out the rule about adding endings to the verbs.
5 What other endings can you add?
6 There are a very small number of **f** nouns that just add **s**. Can you think of them? Check your guesses in the dictionary.
7 Can you hear the **v** in the words that change? Try saying the words.

Double **f**	Single **f**	**fe**	Exceptions
stuff	scarf	wife	chiefs
cliff	wolf	knife	dwarfs
cuff	calf	life	roofs
dandruff	leaf	safe	reefs
staff	shelf		briefs
sniff	self		
scuff	elf		
bluff	loaf		
handcuff	half		
fluff	deaf		

Notes
◆ Plurals
  ◆ **ff** – add **s**;
  ◆ **f** and **fe** – change to **ves**.

◆ Verbs
  ◆ **ff** – just add the ending (e.g. *bluffs*);
  ◆ **f** – change to **v** and add ending (e.g. *halving*);
  ◆ **fe** – change to **v**, drop the **e**, add the ending (e.g. *saves*).

◆ Other endings
  ◆ Just add **y** or **ish** (e.g. *fluffy*, *selfish*);
  ◆ An interesting one: *mischievous*.

Year 5
Term 3

Objective 5

To investigate and learn spelling rules:
- words ending in **y** preceded by a consonant change **y** to **ie** when adding a suffix, e.g. *flies, tried* – except for the suffixes **ly** or **ing**, e.g. *slyly, flying*

SHARED INVESTIGATION (teacher led)
Adding suffixes to words ending in **y**

Prompts

1. Look at the adjectives in the empty grid. Help me to add suffixes to my first word, *happy*.
2. Now we've done a few, can you see any rules about adding suffixes to adjectives ending in **y**?
3. Can you think of other adjectives ending in **y** (e.g. *hungry, lazy*). Does it work for them?
4. Let's try it with verbs ending in **y**. What suffixes could we add?
5. You should be able to spot an exception here. Why would it be odd if we changed **y** to **i** when we add **ing**?
6. Can you think of other verbs? Does the rule hold good for them? (*cry, fly, reply*).

Adjective	ness	er	est	ly
happy	happiness	happier	happiest	happily
pretty	prettiness	prettier	prettiest	prettily
lazy	laziness	lazier	laziest	lazily

Verb	ing	ed			
marry	marrying	married	marriage		
try	trying	tried	trial		
vary	varying	varied	variation	variable	variety

Notes

- Change **y** to **i** when you add a suffix.
- Two important exceptions:
  - keep the **y** when you add **ing** (can't have two **i**s together);
  - with words ending in vowel + consonant keep the **y** (can't have three vowels together);
- There are more varied suffixes for verbs.

Year 5
Term 1

Objective 8

To identify word roots, derivations and spelling patterns, e.g. *sign, signature, signal; bomb, bombastic, bombard; remit, permit, permission*, in order to extend vocabulary and provide support for spelling

INDEPENDENT INVESTIGATION (working without the teacher)
To identify word roots, derivations and spelling patterns

Prompts

1   Find as many words as you can that include the word *sign*.
    – In what sense do these words contain the meaning of the word *sign*?
    – Say the words out loud. Circle the words in which the **g** is silent.
    – Remembering the family of words will remind you to put in the **g**.
2   Repeat this activity with the other words – *bomb, muscle, medicine, finite, music, front, part* and *script*.
    – Explain how the words are linked in meaning.
    – Look for differences in the way the words are sounded out.
    – How can the word families help you with spellings?
3   Find other families of words linked by meaning and spelling.
4   Find other examples of silent or quiet letters which are sounded out by other words in the word family.

sign	signal	significant	signpost	signature	signify
spectacle	inspection	spectator	spectacular	spectrum	retrospect
bomb	bombastic	bombardier			
muscle	muscular				
medicine	medical	medicinal			
finite	infinity	definite	finish	final	
music	musician	musical			
front	frontier				
part	partial	partition	particular	partake	participate
script	scripture	description	prescription	manuscript	postscript

Notes

◆ Family words sometimes sound out silent letters, e.g. *sign – signature*.
◆ Family words can sometimes clarify unstressed or quiet letters, e.g. the second **i** in *definite*.

Year 6
Term 1

Objective 5

To use word roots, prefixes and suffixes as a support for spellings, e.g. **aero**, **aqua**, **audi**, **bi**, **cede**, **clude**, **con**, **cred**, **duo**, **log(o)(y)**, **hyd(ro)(ra)**, **in**, **micro**, **oct**, **photo**, **port**, **prim**, **scribe**, **scope**, **sub**, **tele**, **tri**, **ex**

SHARED INVESTIGATION (teacher led)
To use word roots, prefixes and suffixes as a support for spelling

Prompts

1 Here are four words starting with **bi**. What do they mean? If I told you that **bi** means a certain number, can you work out what the number is? It was once a Greek word, which we borrowed. Can you think of any more words containing **bi**?

2 Here are four words starting with **aqua**. Can you work out what **aqua** means? Tell us how you worked it out. Can you think of other words with **aqua** in them?

3 Think about the word **super**. It was once a Latin word for 'greater'. Can you think of any words with **super** in them? Why do they mean 'greater'?

4 Here are some more examples to work out ...

5 What other roots can you spot in our list of words? (**cycle**, **ped**, **nova**, **bio**, **geo**, **phon**, **visi**). How can we work out their meanings?

Some useful examples to start with:				
bi	*two*	bicycle	biped	binoculars	binary
aqua	*water*	aquarium	Aquarius	aquatic	aquaplane
super	*greater*	supernatural	Superman	supernova	superpower
port	*carry*	transport	portable	import	export
trans	*across*	transport	transplant	transfer	transaction
auto	*self*	automatic	autograph	autobiography	automobile
phobia	*fear*	claustrophobia	arachnophobia	agoraphobia	xenophobia
ology	*study*	archaeology	biology	geology	zoology
tele	*far off*	telephone	television	telepathy	telecom

Notes

◆ Word roots' spellings are generally reliable, so they are useful for spelling. The word *bicycle* is a good example – the roots clarify where to place the **i** and **y**.

◆ Build on from here by using the common prefixes and suffixes, e.g. **re**, **pre**, **able**, etc.

Year 6
Term 1/2/3

Objective 4

Revise and extend work on spelling patterns for unstressed vowels in polysyllabic words from Year 5 Term 3

INDEPENDENT INVESTIGATION (working without the teacher)
Revise the best way to spell unstressed vowels in polysyllabic words

Prompts

1 Some vowels are difficult to make out because they are spoken quickly or quietly. The 'beat' in the word falls elsewhere, so they don't sound out clearly.

2 Write in a list the words *separate, definite, vegetable*, and *parliament*. Put a circle round the vowel that is hard to hear. Discuss how people in your group remember the correct spelling, and make a list of useful suggestions such as:
   – saying it as it might sound if the vowel was *clear* (*Parli – aaah! – ment*);
   – linking it to words in the same family (definite – finite, infinity);
   – finding words within words (*get* in *vegetable*);
   – making up a mnemonic (memory trick).

3 Look for more examples in the days of the week and the months of the year.

4 Look for more examples in your own writing or spelling log.

5 Find a way of remembering the unstressed vowel in each of your tricky words. Make an A4 wall poster for each one, to share with the rest of the class.

6 Look for words in which a consonant is hard to hear (e.g. *handbag, government*). What causes consonants to go quiet, and how can you remember them?

Unstressed vowels					Unstressed consonants
definite	separate	jewellery	skeleton	miniature	Wednesday
vegetable	parliament	benefit	locomotive	journalist	February
fattening	corporal	margarine	signature	Saturday	environment
astronomy	January	February	medicine	geography	government
dandelion	lemonade	alcohol	secretary	grammar	handbag
holiday	mathematics	history	lettuce	television	cupboard
telephone	parallel	consonant	similar	describe	raspberry

Appendix 4
Differentiation issues

Have a clear plan for what children must, should and could learn, e.g.:
◆ *must* learn to add a simple suffix to the end of a word;
◆ *should* learn to change **y** to **i**, and to drop the final **e** where appropriate;
◆ *could* learn to retain the **e** which keeps **c** and **g** soft.

Stage and direct the questions to stretch children at their own level.

To give extra support:
◆ Allow thinking time to engage less confident children.
◆ Ask open questions which will allow you to take different levels of contribution.
◆ Encourage additional adults to drop clues, but not answers.
◆ Precede the lesson with a preparation activity for weaker groups.
◆ Allocate time for consolidation work.

To extend:
◆ Take the investigation further, e.g. find exceptions, find similar rules, apply to other words.
◆ Set challenging investigations for able groups in independent time.
◆ Invite able groups to design, collect words and run an investigation with the rest of the class.

Appendix 5
Whole-class consolidation activities

◆ 'Show me' cards

To each child, distribute cards with which they will indicate choices, e.g. **s** or **es**. When you provide a word, they show you the card they think is correct. This strategy obliges every child to pay attention and participate. The teacher can see at a glance who has understood the rule and who has not.

◆ Individual whiteboards

Each child has a whiteboard (these can be made by laminating A4 white card). The cards can be used to practise and show spellings, perhaps examples already flashed and hidden by the teacher. Alternatively, they can be used to try out rules on new words, and then shown simultaneously to the teacher. Whiteboards are good for participation, brainstorming and at-a-glance assessment.

◆ Postboxes

Two trays or boxes are used to sort cards. For example, a **rainbow** box and a **cow** box could be used to collect cards for different pronunciations of **ow**. A set of cards can be distributed among members of the class ready for posting, and later, the postbox can be emptied to look for patterns.

◆ Human words

Each child has a letter card, and children stand in line to create words. Spelling transformations can then be made by other children carrying, for example, an apostrophe. Another version of this uses base words with which different compound words can be formed.

YEAR 3   TERM 1

Objective	Activity
8	Whiteboards to try new **ing** spellings once the pattern has been taught.
9	Whiteboards to try new **le** spellings once the pattern has been taught.
10–11	'Show me' cards and/or postboxes for **dis**, **un**, and **anti** and other comparable prefixes.

YEAR 3   TERM 2

Objective	Activity
9	'Show me' cards for **s** or **es** endings.
10	Letter fans or whiteboards indicating the silent letter in response to spoken word or flashcard.
11	'Show me' cards for singular and plural words.
12–14	Cards or whiteboards containing words to join up into compounds.
15	Line up children holding whiteboard letters to create words such as *cannot* and ask an 'apostrophe' child to create a space for themselves by replacing other children.

YEAR 3   TERM 3

Objective	Activity
8	Use whiteboards or wall posters to collect up examples of words within words.
9–10	'Show me' cards or postboxes for **dis**, **un**, and **anti** and other comparable prefixes.
11	Line up children holding whiteboard letters and ask an 'apostrophe' child to create a space for themselves.

YEAR 4   TERM 1

Objective	Activity
6	'Show me' cards for homophones.
7	Whiteboards to attempt the extension of words.
9	Suffix postboxes into which suitable words are posted, and then scanned for patterns and rules.
10	Whiteboards for spot test of key words.

YEAR 4   TERM 2

Objective	Activity
5	'Show me' cards for **s** and **ves**.
6	Postboxes or wall poster to collect up words with common strings over a period of time. Children try to guess which will collect most. Try **ight**, **tch**, **ough**, **ought**, **ould**.
7	Whiteboards for spot test of key words.

YEAR 4   TERM 3

Objective	Activity
6	Postboxes to sort different pronunciations, e.g. *rainbow, flower*.
7	Whiteboards or wall posters to brainstorm lists of words using the same root, e.g. *press*.
8	Cards or whiteboards containing word parts to join up into compounds.
9	'Show me' cards for close suffixes, e.g. **able**, **ible**, **tion** and **sion**.
10	'Show me' cards for *its* and *it's* in response to a spoken sentence.

YEAR 5   TERM 1

Objective	Activity
5	'Show me' cards for suffix choices, e.g. **s** or **es**, **ys** or **ies**, **fs** or **ves**.
6	Use whiteboards or wall posters to collect up words using the same root, e.g. *sign, bomb*.

YEAR 5   TERM 2

Objective	Activity
5	Postboxes to sort words with different pronunciations, e.g. b<u>oo</u>t, f<u>oo</u>t.
6	'Show me' cards for homophones in spoken sentences.
7	'Show me' cards for *their/theirs* in response to spoken sentences.
8	Postboxes or wall posters for words which use different suffixes, e.g. **cian**, **sion** and **tion**, then study contents to find patterns, e.g. words ending in **c** use **cian**; most words use **tion**; words ending in **de** or **s** use **sion**.

YEAR 5   TERM 3

Objective	Activity
4	Letter fans (vowels only) for identifying the unstressed vowel in a spoken word.
5	Use whiteboards to form modified words and show them, e.g. *energy – energise*.

YEAR 6   TERM 1

Objective	Activity
4	Letter fans (vowels only) for identifying the unstressed vowel in a spoken word.
5	Postboxes, whiteboards or wall posters to collect up words using the same root, prefix or suffix in order to find patterns and deduce meanings.
6	Cards or whiteboards containing word parts to join up into compounds.

YEAR 6   TERM 2

Objective	Activity
4	Wall posters for handy mnemonics. Letter fans (vowels only) for identifying the unstressed vowel in a spoken word.

YEAR 6   TERM 3

Objective	Activity
4	Wall posters for handy mnemonics. Letter fans (vowels only) for identifying the unstressed vowel in a spoken word.

Appendix 6
Spelling journals

A number of children are now successfully using spelling journals as a self-help device and a place to record their work on spelling. The journal can include:

◆ a log of personal errors;
◆ personal spelling lists to learn;
◆ aides-memoire of spelling conventions;
◆ working out from spelling investigations;
◆ dictionary of high frequency words learnt/unlearnt;
◆ spelling targets;
◆ spelling 'tries';
◆ tests.

Extracts from spelling journals

The following pages show a number of extracts from spelling journals.

1. Creating mnemonic phrases for tricky words
2. Applying a spelling convention taught in shared time
3. A list of words to learn, identified by child from own work
4. Investigating different ways of making the long **o** sound
5. Investigating different ways of making the long **a** sound
6. A brainstorm of collective nouns
7. A brainstorm of words derived from given roots
8. A spelling competition based on car number plates
9. A record of meanings of root words
10. Finding words within words
11. Using a dictionary to apply prefixes
12. Using a dictionary to find words using a given prefix

Special thanks to:
Jane Walters, Literacy Consultant, West Sussex LEA
Manor Hall County Middle School, Southwick
Edward Bryant Primary School, Bognor Regis

1.

Friday 19th Sep '97

Mnemonics

Ought
Oh ugly giraffe how tall.

Because
big elephants can always upset
small elephants
Beautiful
beautiful Ella always uses
turquaise in for unusual letters.
Rhythm.
Rhythm has your toes hopping
madly.
Enchantress
Every noble child has a nice
teacher roughly educated
successfully styled.
People
Pandas everywhere over pampered
love eating.
typical.

✓

77

2.

Plurals
Rule 1   12.10.48

~~Plurals rule 1.~~

You can hear when you have to write es because you add on extra syllables.

Pen - Pens
Box - Boxes
~~Cow - Cows~~
House - Houses (Exception)
Glass - Glasses
Fox = Foxes
Fin - Fins
Bus - Buses
Class - Classes
Case - Cases (Exception)

✓

3.

My Words to learn:

17, 5, 1999

1. Could

2. Would

3. Might

4. Started

5. Stopped

6. through

7. ~~throught~~ thought

8. told

9. tries

10. Walked ✓

4.

Wednesday   21st April

The Long 'O' sothds

Oa	O-e	Ow
goal	bone	Show
Goalk×	home	Slowing
Cool	throne	mow
loan	gote	
goat		

5.

Wednesday 24th February.

The long vowel
<u>a</u>

a	gaze	Strange
Sale	grace	grate
train	table	away
make	lace	Lady
Space	play	
? (back)	mermaid	Well done
(Having)	wednsday	- you have
day	windsday	found a
came	maze	huge number in
wait	Kate	a short time.
plain	Same	
cage	chocolate	
grape	acre	
Jake	table	
James	potato	
Shape	lady bird	
face	cabbage	
race	baby	
chase	favourite	

6.

25th February 1999

1 flock 10 pack

2 floor

3 liver

4 gaggle collective nouns

5 library

6

6 pride

7 band

8 bouquet

9 forest

7.

Sign: Signal
Signet
Signalman
Signatory
Signature
Significance
Signify
Significant
Signpost

Just: Justice
Justify
Justifiable

Like: Likely
Likeable
Liklihood
Liken
Likeness
~~Likewise~~
Likewise
Liking

✓

Kind: Kindergarten
Kindle
Kindling
Kindly
Kindred

Friend: Friendly
Friendship
Friendless
Friendliness

Avail: Available

Excellent 3 hpts.

83

8.

Car Number Plates
Thursday 22nd January '98

Use the letters to make a word. They must be
in the same order.
eg   BTE - absolute
        - bite

Enl - england
Ech - eachother - Speech
Sta - Station
Nts - Nuts
Bkg - Biking
Kkg - Kicking
Oah - Coach
Rgt - Ragt - Drigt
Mgl - Muffeled
Nml - Animal - normal
KCN - Kichen Kitchen   TDY - tidy
CHR - chair - children   CRM - creamy
BRK - bark - break
BLD - bald - blood
SND - sand - sneered
CLK - chalk -   ✓
YLW - yellow
GDB - goodbye

9.

Tuesday 30th June 1998

Making compound Words from Greek roots

Greek Root	Meaning
tele	far off
peri	around
micro	small
phone	voice
mega	great
stetha	chest
photo	light
ghraph	written
scope	look at
geo	earth
book	read
shop	buy from
farm	animals
tele	vision
hand	body
yard	place
writting	use
wash	do-clean
run	energy

10.

1st October 97

Word Hunt

Whatever	manufacturing	manager
what ✓	man ✓	man ✓
hat ✓	fact ✓	age ✓
hate ✓	facturing ✓	a ✓
at ✓	ring ✓	nag ✓
ate ✓	ing	
eve ✓		
ever ✓		

refuse	Intelligent	entirely
fuse ✓	In ✓	I ✓
us ✓	tell ✓	tire ✓
use ✓	gent ✓	

knowledge	Preacher	Stranger
know ✓	reach ✓	strange ✓
now ✓	her ✓	ran ✓
led ✓	ache ✓	rang ✓
edge ✓	each ✓	anger ✓
	Preach ✓	

✓ super work

11.

Prefix

1.10.97

Word	Prefix + word	Meaning of the new word
Take	mistake	something taken (DOEN) wrong.
Lead	mislead	To give somebody a wrong idea
agree	disagree	to have a different opinion
qualify	disqualify	Bar someone a competition
approve	disapprove	Not to approve of someone or something
pleasure	displeasure	To annoy.
Satisfaction	dissatisfaction	Not satisfied
Service	disservice	A harmful action
Solve	dissolve	Mix something with a liquid so it is a li
Similar	dissimilar	Things that aren't the same
appear	dissappear	To vanish
appoint	dissappoint	Not happy with someone.
hear	misshear	Didn't hear something.
direct		
(2HP)	You have obviously understood this used the dictionary to good effect -	Crystal and well done.

12.

Word Beginnings

Tri

Trial	tripper
Triangle	tripe
Triangular	Triple
Tribe	triplet
Tribal	triplicate
Tribulation	tripod
Tribunal	trite
Tributary	triumph
Tribute	triumphant
Trick	trivial
Trickle	
Tricycle	
trident	
triple	
trifling	
trigger	
trigonometry	
trill	
trim	
trimming	
trinket	
trio	
trip	

✓ 33 good 'tri' words

Crystal – well done (IHP)